CRE▲TIVE
HOMEOWNER®

can't fail color
schemes

KITCHENS & BATHS

CAN'T FAIL COLOR SCHEMES: KITCHENS & BATHS

SENIOR EDITOR	Kathie Robitz
GRAPHIC DESIGNER	Stephanie Phelan
JUNIOR EDITOR	Jennifer Calvert
PHOTO RESEARCHER	Robyn Poplasky
EDITORIAL ASSISTANT	Nora Grace
DIGITAL IMAGING SPECIALIST	Frank Dyer
INDEXER	Schroeder Indexing Services
COVER DESIGN	Glee Barre
FRONT COVER PHOTOGRAPHY	*top left* Bob Greenspan, stylist: Susan Andrews; *top right* Eric Roth; *bottom left* Mark Samu; *bottom right* Anne Gummerson
INSIDE FRONT COVER PHOTOGRAPHY	courtesy of Sensa by Cosentino
BACK COVER PHOTOGRAPHY	*top* Mark Lohman; *both bottom* courtesy of Merillat
INSIDE BACK COVER PHOTOGRAPHY	Daniel Epstein

CREATIVE HOMEOWNER

VICE PRESIDENT AND PUBLISHER	Timothy O. Bakke
PRODUCTION DIRECTOR	Kimberly H. Vivas
ART DIRECTOR	David Geer
MANAGING EDITOR	Fran J. Donegan

Current Printing (last digit)
10 9 8 7 6 5 4 3 2 1

Can't Fail Color Schemes: Kitchens & Baths, First Edition
Library of Congress Control Number: 2007942948
ISBN-10: 1-578011-413-X
ISBN-13: 978-1-58011-413-4

CREATIVE HOMEOWNER®
A Division of Federal Marketing Corp.
24 Park Way
Upper Saddle River, NJ 07458
www.creativehomeowner.com

dedication

This book is dedicated to my artistic family: Denis, Isaac, Elias, Haniya, and my parents Ruth and Stanley who are all color enthusiasts at heart!

acknowledgments

I would especially like to thank Kathie Robitz, whose insight and expertise are invaluable, Stephanie Phelan, whose art direction is done with her own remarkable sense of style, and all of those who worked so hard on creating this book. I also want to thank the many homeowners who graciously opened up their homes and let us photograph their worlds.

contents

more adventures in
color

E veryone knows that kitchens and bathrooms have become deal makers—or breakers—in today's real estate market. Innovations in design have made these two rooms as much about style as they are about utility. They are the new "power couple." Glamorous materials have helped to make kitchens and baths in even modest homes chic and sophisticated. But investing in costly materials, such as stone and tile, and even costlier cabinets, means taking the time to make careful choices, especially when it comes to color. If you are thinking, "How can I go wrong if I chose all neutral fixtures and materials for my bath?" think again. In the world of beiges, tans, and taupes, there are many variations and some of them clash. Besides, you might be

surprised at how much real color can add to a kitchen or bath if you know how to choose the right ones.

I have always believed that the kitchen is one of the most important rooms in the house. It is the place where family and dear friends gather, talk, relax, cook, and perhaps enjoy a glass of wine at the end of a long day. So the kitchen should look its best and make you feel good as you spend time living in it. Color can do a lot for your mood, whether you are rushing to put a quick meal on the table or enjoying a lively conversation during dinner. It can also help to visually tie together all of the elements, materials, and surfaces in the room, right down to the metallic finish on your cabinet hardware.

The bathrooms in your home are equally important and deserve as much color attention as any other room. I like my bathroom to be a quiet sanctuary, used as much for relaxation as it is for grooming and cleanliness. Other people may want the bathroom to be a cheery place that gets everybody up and out the door in the morning.

Because most homes have more than one bath, design and color choices depend on who is using the room. A master bath like mine might be more low-key; a child's bath might look whimsical; and a teen's bath might reflect some of the fun, trendy colors that attract this age group. The goal is to create a pleasing, personal scheme.

Selecting the colors for your kitchen and bathrooms may be challenging because of the variety of palettes in the world of natural materials and the seemingly limitless number of rich choices in the universe of man-made products and surfaces. Complicating that even further is the effect of texture and finishes on color; it can range from smooth to rough, and shiny to matte—all in the same room.

Each of these materials has characteristics that make them appealing and practical for your lifestyle. *Can't Fail Color Schemes: Kitchens & Baths* will help you choose the right colors for them. Once you decide on a direction, stick with it, and have fun along the way!

Part 1

making the right CHOICES

from **bland**

*See how color can add personality to
your kitchen and bath*

When you look at the colors in your kitchen or bath, do you love them? Do you feel that they are a reflection of your personal taste? Do they elicit the right mood? If the answer is no, it's time for a change.

Color choices are always important to a design, and the right ones can make a kitchen more appealing and a bath more personal. For example, energetic reds and oranges can stimulate the appetite and put people in a sociable mood—perfect hues for a gathering spot like the kitchen. On the other hand, earthy neutrals can have a calming effect, which may be just right for a low-key master bath. Study the rooms on the following pages, and think of how you can change the look and feel of your kitchen and bath with color.

the meaning of color

*Each color has the power to affect the mood
of a room in different ways. How do you
want your kitchen or bath to feel?*

Red

Red is the color that stimulates the strongest emotional response. A powerful color, luscious red can be exciting and take center stage in any room design. Cherry red is an energetic color symbolizing romance, whereas earthy brick red has the warmth of an earth tone with an understated, classic look. Deep reds have a traditional feeling of importance and stature, and bright reds impart the feeling of daring adventure. Either way, red will attract the most attention—whether it is used as a wall or an accent color.

Orange

Orange is the color of enthusiasm. Orange can range from bright yellow-oranges to deep terra-cotta and rust. The orange family of colors relays the refreshing feeling of fun and warmth. As a bright yellow-orange, the light-hearted feeling of energetic orange is fun and youthful. Rich oranges can be terra-cotta or darker brick orange, which remarkably share the warmth of an earth tone. Used as a dominant color in your design, light orange can be cheerful and whimsical, while a rich-orange theme can be nutty and comforting.

Yellow

When people think of yellow, they think of sunshine. Bright and enthusiastic, yellow can be an optimistic color that is upbeat and bright eyed. The more delicate, lighter wheat tones can be comforting because of their easy-on-the-eyes subtle hues. Coordinating with almost any other color, soft yellows have a homey quality that makes them easy with which to live. Bright yellows, on the other hand, can have a vibrating intensity that can be difficult on the eyes. Because of the saturated quality of intense yellows, they can make young children agitated if overused.

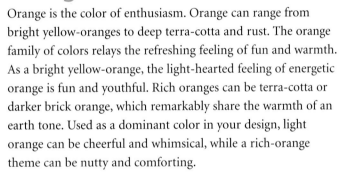

Green

Green is a comfort color. Relaxing and soothing, green is used in places where people are comforted, whether it is a medical facility or a "green room" where people relax before a performance. Lighter soft greens recall nature and soothing earth tones, while dark greens inspire a more conservative, traditional environment. Although usually considered a color that is calming, new versions of green have a feeling of renewal and youthful enthusiasm. These lime and neon greens are playful and energetic. They are fun and cheerful for the young at heart.

Blue

"True blue" is an expression that describes the qualities of loyalty and honesty. That is the color blue. The color of water and the sky, blue denotes integrity. Most popular in bedrooms, this color can be a cool blue-gray or a baby blue, which is restful and calming. One of the most-popular colors, blue generally has a refreshing sense of tranquility. Although some find darker gray-blue to be somber—hence the term, "feeling blue"—it is most often thought of as a "blue-ribbon" color, implying that it is the best there is.

Purple

Rich, deep purples call to mind luxury and wealth. The color associated with royalty, purple denotes a luxurious sense of sophistication. Rich purples are often used in rooms with a quiet elegance, whereas light purples, such as lilac and lavender, are used to convey a light-hearted or romantic feeling. Soft purples can be more feminine than the richer tones of the color, which can create a feeling of splendor and style when you use it sparingly. Whether a whimsical accent for yellows and oranges or a majestic accompaniment to warm earth tones, purples can set the stage for a room.

Brown

The color of nature and the earth underfoot, brown has the feeling of stability and security. A reliable color that ranges from gentle earthy beige and brown-gray taupe to rich chocolaty brown, this earth tone has a sense of timelessness. A mellow and cozy color, the down-to-earth browns recall the luscious textures of wood and leather. The soft tones can be quiet and conservative, the backdrop to any palette, whereas rich browns give the feeling of balance and strength. With the warmth of cocoa and coffee, browns can be hearty and comforting.

Black

Black is the color of understated elegance. A serious color, black has a sense of strength in design. Used as the dominant color in a room, black presents a sense of power and prestige. Overpowering if overused, ebony black can be the perfect backdrop to contrasting colors and metallic accents. Softened by the use of a deep charcoal color or less-saturated lighter grays, the classic black family will complement any color. However, the stature of true black will always embody the style and class of a black-tie affair.

White

Snowy white is the purest color. Bright white gives the feeling of freshness. Reflecting light, bright white enriches the more colorful tones with a strong contrast. Off-whites can bring in more warmth—creamy and pearl-colored whites have a warm glow, for example. Pastel hues paired with a soft white can be a soothing combination, whereas richer colors look crisp and clear alongside clean white. Whether you're working with the earthier ivory variations or pure bright white, either choice complements the palette with a sense of clarity and freshness.

how we perceive color

Believe it or not, everyone sees color a little differently. What used to be called **color blindness** is actually a **color deficiency**. Almost everyone sees some color; it is a matter of how much color they see. About 12 percent of men and 0.5 percent of women have some degree of color deficiency. "Is the traffic light red or green?" "Am I sunburned? I can't see the red in my skin." "That bush has flowers on it? I don't see any!" These are the kinds of things someone might say who has trouble seeing certain colors.

Your eyes have three **color receptors,** called **cones,** that give you the ability to perceive different wavelengths of light, which translates to color recognition in your brain. People who cannot see the full spectrum of colors have a deficiency of one or more of these cones. The most prevalent

what do you see?

Here are two examples of how some people see a colorful kitchen, left, and how others may see the same room differently, right.

If you see pink, doesn't everyone see pink? Not necessarily.

is the inability to see the difference between reds and greens. This is far more common than people realize. A person may be wearing a pink sweater, but her friend sees that sweater as a perfect shade of khaki. The friend does not realize that he is seeing the color differently. When choosing a wall color, make sure everyone is happy with the final choice, however they see it!

What is less common is the inability to differentiate between blues and yellows. Lastly, some people are not capable of seeing any color, only shades of gray. However, this condition is rare. "Color Deficiency" is a condition from birth and is mostly inherited. So remember, color-deficient people can't help what they see—and they don't always know that they see colors differently than others.

the differences

There are three ways that people can be color deficient. An easy way to categorize people's color deficiency is the following: **red-weak, green-weak,** or **blue-weak**. Each color-deficient person will perceive the colors in their own way. Here are some examples of what these people see.

color	as seen by the color-deficient
bright red	olive green to yellow to orange
true green	bright yellow to taupe to turquoise
blue/purple	gray blue to brown blue to rust

putting light

on the subject

How lighting affects color

When deciding what colors will look best in the kitchen or bath—or any room for that matter—keep in mind the color of the lighting.

Different sources of light can affect how a room's colors look and how they make you feel.

An **incandescent** bulb, which is a common household light source, adds warmth to a room. Simple off-white will appear more golden when it is illuminated by only an incandescent bulb. A stronger yellow room, bright in day-

ABOVE: Lighting that is closest to sunlight is best for grooming.

OPPOSITE: Warm incandescent lighting enhances this kitchen's wood tones.

light, will look somewhat softer in the evening when the light bulbs soak up the intensity of the yellow. Deep red will appear to be brick red; blue will look slightly green; and cool gray will seem to be warmer taupe.

The incandescent light that you use for most of your indoor lighting needs is perfect for rooms where you look at and groom yourself, such as the bath. Your complexion will appear healthier and more attractive in the bathroom mirror under soft, warm incandescence.

The standard **fluorescent** bulb, on the other hand, adds a cool-spectrum cast, an ultraviolet or blue tinge to the colors in the room. Warm wall colors—yellow, gold, orange, wheat tones—lose their warmth in standard fluorescent light. Yellow appears yellow-green, red looks like purple, and skin tone has a blue-gray

ABOVE: Soft candlelight next to the tub will make you feel pampered. **OPPOSITE:** A variety of lighting types increases the function and look of this kitchen.

ABOVE: The shade or covering over a bulb will affect the light. All three styles here diffuse and soften the illumination.

cast. It is as if these colors have been "washed" with a subtle blue overtone. Because of its unflattering nature, it is generally not recommended for indoors, except for some task lighting. However, newer warm white fluorescents are truer to natural light and don't have the cold blue cast of the old standard fluorescent.

A halogen bulb gives off a bright white light that closely resembles the qualities of daylight. The intensity of the heat produced by a halogen bulb means that you have to be careful where you place it. However, its crisp light provides excellent task lighting. A compact, low-voltage version of halogen is perfect for

accent lighting. Because of the balanced purity of the halogen light, artwork, such as oil paintings, photographs, and sculpture, look true to life within its remarkable glow. Therefore, low-voltage halogen lighting is the perfect choice for museums and art galleries, allowing viewers to appreciate the true colors and textures of what is on display.

The most minimal, soothing light source is **candlelight**. Nothing comes close to the warm glow of the candle's flame to create a serene atmosphere. Whether it is a lit candelabra on the table or small tea lights on the ledge of the tub, warm, glowing candlelight creates a cozy and luxurious mood in any room.

Lastly, consider whether your lighting choice enhances the colors in the room. Your eyes will compensate or adjust for

OPPOSITE: In this family bath, deep-red walls pick up the reddish tones in the room's wood flooring.

the yellow glow or blue cast in the room, but is the amount of light right for the space? The more-saturated wall colors, a deep purple or an intense red, will actually absorb rather than reflect the light, requiring more light to illuminate your room.

On the other hand, lighter colors will reflect light and brighten a space.

You can also make light bounce off the ceiling to highlight its accent color or to add softer reflected light.

It is crucial to incorporate adequate lighting for your needs. Maximize your home's exposure to **natural sunlight** in order to keep spaces bright and upbeat.

Allowing fresh air and natural sunlight to dapple your kitchen encourages a cheerful mood. Natural light, more than any lightbulb, creates a mood of overall wellness that cannot be imitated by an artificial light source over the tub or on the side of the vanity.

ABOVE: Take color cues from permanent features, such as kitchen cabinets.
OPPOSITE: Soften a bright sun-filled room with a muted wall color.

out of the woods

selecting the right color for wood

Wood and wood finishes will have a big impact on the overall color scheme, style, and mood of your kitchen or bath. Dark, grainy woods look more traditional while lighter woods with a tighter grain appear sleek and modern. Mid-range tones are more versatile, but when the grain and texture is prominent, the wood has a warmer country appeal.

Selecting a type of wood goes hand in hand with choosing a stain—which is what adds the color—unless you plan to paint. A stain can range from transparent, which allows the grain to show completely, to semitransparent, semiopaque, or opaque satin, which looks a lot like paint.

The darkest wood treatment is an ebony stain—a rich black that can add

Mixing contrasting wood tones—light cabinets and dark floors—adds sophistication to this design.

richness to a less-expensive wood. A Jacobean stain is another deeply saturated color—dark brown—that reveals a minimal amount of grain.

Dark woods tend to look best when they are finished with rich warm stains, frequently those with brown-black undertones, such as deep cherry, walnut, or mahogany. **Cherry** has depth to it; it shows the grain and the natural variations

OPPOSITE: Paint and glaze show off the depth and decorative details of this raised-panel cabinetry. **BELOW:** The honey-colored oak cabinets in this kitchen are warm and versatile. This mid-tone blends easily with many wall and counter treatments.

in it. Second to cherry, is **walnut.** A darker brown with the slightest hint of olive, walnut has less color but it is deep. With a touch of red, **mahogany** is a great choice if you are willing to carry it over to other wood elements in the room—the table and chairs, for example. Perhaps more than cherry and walnut, mahogany is often associated with traditional decor. But if you use it as an accent with a contrasting color, such as light maple, you can achieve a sleek contemporary look.

The mid-range wood colors include classic oak, rustic chestnut, and pine. Each one has its own identity, but all of them are cozy and warm. These mid-range wood colors have a visible grain.

White oak is lighter than red oak, which has hints of red or pink. Both have an open grain. Yellow pine has a strong golden overtone to it. Alder is becoming increasingly popular for cabinets and floors. It has a straight grain, and it ranges in color from the mid-tone reddish-brown to a pale yellow.

The lightest woods, a tight, clear maple for example, are both sleek and dramatic. With the least amount of color, the delicate tone of this wood gives the impression of purity and cleanliness. For a dramatic approach to your design, you might pair white pine with a contrasting color. Used with an alternating ebony black or rich Jacobean stain, the look is as classic as black and white.

In addition to staining, applying a toner can affect the color of wood. The purpose of a toner is to even out a color. This finishing layer can be tinted with a pigment or dye to camouflage imperfections in the wood, such as areas that are brighter or darker or vertical striping that shows where separate sections have been joined.

Glazing is a way of highlighting the architectural qualities of cabinetry. A glaze consists of pigmented stains

The light and dark tones in this kitchen illustrate what you can do to alter wood's color with stain. Here you can see a clear stain next to a pigmented one.

applied to a surface that is sealed. A glaze color that contrasts with the wood brings out details when it sinks into crevices, such as those on molding, the edges of recessed panels on cabinet doors, or the grain in a panel. When you wipe off the glaze, color remains in places you cannot get into with a rag or a brush.

Pickling, or color washing, is another way to alter the color of wood cabinets, floors, paneling, or trimwork. The process involves applying a thinned-down—almost sheer, semiopaque—coat of paint to the wood, letting it soak into the grain, and then wiping it off of the surface. Depending on the color of the paint and the type of wood, it can lighten or darken the appearance and accentuate or play down the grain. Pickling works best with woods that have an open grain. Thinned paint will not soak into wood with a tight grain. Instead, it will merely sit on the surface; once it is wiped, the look is inconsistent. For a contemporary decor, use thinned-down white paint. For a vintage look, try color washing with a deep green, blue, or rich golden hue.

OPPOSITE: The chestnut-stained bead board has a rich patina, adding a vintage feeling to this bathroom. **ABOVE:** Wild graining in the wood enhances the furniture-quality look of this kitchen cabinetry.

irresistible handsome stone

choosing the right stone and color

When it comes to kitchen and bath design, choosing stone for countertops, floors, or even walls definitely will "kick it up a notch." Everyone wants stone today. And why not? It's glamorous and durable, two qualities that increase the beauty and value of a home. Selecting the right stone, however, isn't always easy because it's expensive and permanent. It's also tricky to choose the right color. Even though stone is often neutral, as are most fixtures and appliances, these hues

OPPOSITE: Engineered stone provides the most color options.
BELOW: The blacker the granite, the higher the price.

vary and are hard to match. Because you don't want to make a costly mistake, obtain a sample of the stone you are considering before you place an order. Take it home and look at it in the room and under different lighting conditions. Compare it with other dominant, permanent elements in the room, such as cabinets, tile, and fixtures. If there are flecks or variations of color in the stone, you could pick up one of them in the paint color for the walls or use it as an accent.

Stone is widely popular as a countertop, but you can use it on floors and walls, too, in the form of tile. In that case, get a sample tile and perform the same examination.

The most popular stone, **granite,** is the hardest of the natural-stone products. Its one-of-a-kind quality and remarkable variations in color and pattern define its beauty. Some of the rich blacks, which range from deeply saturated to almost gray-black, sparkle with metallic-like crystalizations, while others can be quiet and understated.

If black isn't your preference, you can easily find granites in all shades, includ-

ABOVE: Classic white marble with light gray veining always looks elegant.
OPPOSITE: The remarkable patterning on this stone makes it the focus of this kitchen.

ing brown and beige as well as green, and blue. More exotic granite colors include pink, red, violet, white, and yellow. It's not unusual to see a combination of hues—gold, peach, cream, and brown—all swirling and running into each other in one slab of granite. Just be careful: if the stone's pattern is busy, it may clash with other elements in the room.

Another rich stone is **marble.** In addition to classic pure white, choices include earthy neutrals from pale cream to chocolate brown and pearl gray to jet black, as well as mid- and dark green tones, faint blush pink, warm rose, deep red, and rich dark green. Veining, typically blue, gray,

or gold, can be feathery light or deeply dramatic. However, marble is a porous stone, making it vulnerable to damaging permanent stains.

A stone with a naturally weathered texture is **limestone.** However, the surface can be polished or honed to make it smooth. Limestone is often a neutral beige tone, but there are some vibrant shades of blue and green, too.

Soapstone is yet another option. Colors include blue-gray, green-gray, dark stone-gray, and tan. Applying a protective coat of mineral oil to the surface deepens its color. Some soapstone has feather-light veins or flecks of green or

blue that complement its subtle palette. Like granite, it is heat and stain resistant.

With its dramatic colors and textures, a handsome alternative to polished stone is **slate**. A rich range of muted grays, gray-greens, slate blues, purples, golden ambers, and browns is consistently earthy and warm. Slate contains several natural minerals, and so a single slab or tile may display more than one color. Slate does

OPPOSITE: This soapstone surface in a soothing tan shows off subtle veining that the polished finish enhances.
ABOVE: These slate tiles display several variations on a gray-green theme.

not absorb stains and is naturally slip and stress resistant. This stone usually has a matte finish, but you can oil the surface for a low-luster effect.

Made from less-than-glamorous stone aggregate, **concrete** has become trendy for countertops, sinks, and tubs, as well as for floors and walls today. This suddenly chic material can be textured or smooth, molded into any shape, and tinted any color, from earthy tones, such as ivory, clay, or beige, to pastels or vivid hues. You can inlay concrete with other materials, such as glass, stone, tile, or metal. This versatile product is also heat and scratch resistant, but it can stain. To

avoid discoloration or damage, sealing or waxing is recommended.

Another alternative to natural stone is is **engineered** or **composite stone.** Most people refer to it simply as "quartz" because, in most cases, that is 95 percent of its contents. (A few manufacturers offer engineered stone that comprises granite chips.) This man-made material is formed by binding the stone chips to powders and resins. The product looks and feels like natural stone, although patterns occurring in nature are more random and less uniform than the ones engineered stone mimics.

The color choices are remarkable, too. Neutrals include natural-looking snowy whites, creams, grays, taupes, blacks, and even rich browns. Lighter pastel colors and deeply saturated shades and tones may include some you will never find in nature—yellow, yellow-gold, orange, fire-engine red, electric blue, and acid green aren't typical of real stone. Some colors come in matte as well as highly polished finishes and in various textures. Engineered stone is stain and scratch resistant, and although it is considered heat resistant, leaving a hot pan on it may cause discoloration.

ABOVE: A sleek concrete countertop has an earthy appeal.
OPPOSITE: This speckled engineered-stone surface mimics the look of natural granite.

man-made laminate materials

plastic laminate and solid surfacing offer a great variety of choices

Decorative laminates, as they are known by kitchen and bath designers, are remarkably durable. In some cases, they can even be a less-expensive solution to your surfacing needs. However, a top-quality plastic laminate and most solid-surfacing material may not only resemble expensive stone, it may be as costly. So what are the benefits? For one thing, the available colors and patterns are much greater—there are over 100 from which to

OPPOSITE: This speckled green surface is only available in a man-made material.
BELOW: A cool neutral color blends beautifully with steel and chrome accents.

choose. That gives you more flexibility when it comes time to select a countertop or a tub or tile surround. Unlike traditional plastic laminate, solid-surfacing material is solid color all the way through it, so you can carve it, rout it, bevel it, or inlay it without creating seams. Both products also offer a number of **looks and textures** that mimic natural materials, such as wood, stone, metal, and leather. They can be smooth, grained, shiny, or matte. Shiny finishes show mars more easily than patterned or matte ones.

Think carefully before you select a color for your laminate surface. It's not easy or inexpensive to change if you make a mis-

take or tire of it. I often think that it's like choosing fabrics that you would wear. If the material is for a kitchen countertop, you'll have to look at it for long periods of time while you prepare meals or even dine, for example. Does that mean you should stick with only neutral colors? Not necessarily.

Certainly if you are thinking about resale value, a neutral color scheme, particularly when it comes to permanent fea-

ABOVE: Like stone, solid surfacing can be carved to create special edge treatments.
OPPOSITE: This speckled black-granite lookalike contrasts well with light woods.

tures, is probably a smart choice. But if you're more interested in creating a look that reflects your personality, choose your colors accordingly. Also keep in mind the other features in the kitchen or bath and how to harmoniously blend them. Especially in the kitchen, choose a countertop color and pattern with the cabinetry in mind. Look at both of them together. It is best to let one of them take center stage while the other serves as a backdrop. For example, I would not suggest using a faux-wood countertop with stained-wood cabinetry. If the cabinet is painted wood, however, you could coordinate it with any solid-color or patterned

laminate counter that you like.

If the cabinets are plain, a bold color or a pattern could make the countertops a focal point in the room. Conversely, if there's a lot going on, you may want to keep the laminate surfaces simple.

What **mood and style** are you going for with the overall design of the room? Deeper hues are typically more traditional, while light colors feel less formal and more contemporary. Again, consider the color of the other elements in the room. Are they warm or cool? Even two whites can be vastly different in temperature.

In fact, there is a wide variety of neutral colors. The beauty of these options is

that they can range from the lightest and most delicate patterns to solid whites, tans, taupes, or beiges to richer browns, grays, and blacks. The warmer, deeper colors lend a cozy feeling, while pale, cool hues look sleek and modern.

To be truly confident about your final selection, you need to see it at home in the location you plan to use it. The small sample chips you find in the store cannot give you an accurate sense of **how a color or pattern will look** on a large countertop or a shower surround. But you can see if it coordinates with other colors, especially if you compare them during different times of the day and in various lighting situations—look at a

countertop sample with the undercabi-net lights turned on, for example. If those lights are compact fluorescents, they will skew the color, making it look somewhat bluer or cooler. Incandescent lights will add a touch of yellow or warmth, and halogen lights, which are whiter, will affect the color the least.

Some laminate manufacturers have interactive Web sites that let you see how different countertop colors look with various cabinets.

ABOVE: The brushed-nickel faucet picks up a tone in the solid-surface countertop.
OPPOSITE: Subtle texture and a warm color complement a traditional design.

styles for tile

decorative tile can make a statement in your design

Because there are so many tile types, styles, and colors, deciding on what to use can be a bit overwhelming. Although tile is generally used to cover large surfaces, such as walls and floors, that will be exposed to moisture, you can also use it to add a touch of color to smaller areas, including backsplashes, counter-tops, and even range hoods. Or use colorful tile to create a design focal point as a wall mural or a mosaic above a cooktop or

BELOW: A band of handpainted Italian tile dresses up a simple blue backsplash.
OPPOSITE: Crisp white and sunny yellow tiles create an upbeat mood.

sink, as an accent in combination with another flooring material, or as a surround for a fireplace opening. Even in small doses, tile can establish a style and introduce color and pattern into a room.

Before you shop for tile, it's wise to become familiar with the number of options available, including ceramic, porcelain, stone, glass, and metal.

Basically, ceramic tile is made from red

OPPOSITE: Handmade Mexican tile sets the tone for this rustic kitchen.
ABOVE: A relaxing scheme of blue and white suits this custom shower.

or white clay that is fired in a kiln and then coated with a durable glaze. Besides sealing the tile, the glaze adds color and pattern to the surface. Porcelain tile is primarily composed of extremely fine or sandlike clay particles that are compressed and baked at an even higher temperature than ceramic tile. Porcelain tile may or may not be glazed.

It you want to expand your porcelain-tile color choices, look into glazed versions, which are more prevalent than in the past. But keep in mind that unlike full-body tile, the color will only be on the surface, so chips will be more appar-

ent. Glazed tile does not require sealing.

Imported Italian, Portuguese, or Mexican tiles are other options. Their brilliant colors and dynamic patterns are popular for backsplashes and counter-tops. Because these tiles are thick, they are excellent for flooring applications, in particular the natural-clay colors—typically deep brick, rich brown, or light taupe. A grout color that will come as close as possible to the color of a natural tile will make the rustic irregularities of the edges less apparent.

Stone tile, cut from slabs of granite, marble, slate, onyx, travertine, or lime-stone, can range in color from deep shades of black, brown, or green to gray, taupe, gold, cream, or white. Some stone, such as marble and granite, can be smooth and luminous, while slate or limestone may have an irregular or rough matte texture.

What is so appealing about natural stone is the unique variations in its patterns (veining). Even stone's imperfections can enhance its inherent natural beauty. However, if you are looking for strict uniformity in color, pattern, and texture, shop for something else.

ABOVE: The neutral tones of the stone tile here have a calming effect.
OPPOSITE: Mosaic tiles pick up other colors in the kitchen to create a cohesive look.

Should you decide to go with stone tile, be sure to inspect multiple samples of your choice to ensure your satisfaction with the variations. Open the boxes and look at each tile carefully.

Depending on your kitchen or bath's overall style—in broad terms, formal or informal—you may want the tile to have a smooth eggshell-like finish or a slightly coarse surface. You can also select a tumbled or antique finish. Tumbling creates chips, indentations, and slightly irregular edges. Sometimes an antique look can be applied to rounded edges to make tile appear worn by age.

Pebble tile is another stone option. It comes with either a polished or matte finish. The small, rounded mesh-backed stones allude to the look of a natural riverbed, making them particularly attractive on the floor of a shower.

Most polished-tile surfaces can achieve a glasslike smoothness that allows light to refract, giving the front of the tile a visible sheen. The depth and luster of this finish is eye-catching.

For a bit of sparkle and glamour in your kitchen or bath, check out metal and glass tiles. You can find copper, bronze, nickel, aluminum, stainless-steel, and pewter tile—in a polished, matte, or antique finish—to coordinate with a kitchen or bathroom's fixtures, hardware, and even the appliances. Many are suitable

for floor as well as wall applications. Moreover, metal is chic with either a modern or a classic interior.

Dazzling with color, glass tile adds a delightful accent to any decor. Fancier and richer in color than natural stone, glass tile can be used on the wall or a countertop, but it's not recommeded for the floor. You can also mix glass with other types of tile. It is the perfect luminous foil for a soft-colored stone, for example. The available colors are endless, including shimmering iridescent versions. Sea glass, which comes in a softer blue-green, has a frosted, tumbled appearance that is perfect as an accent or a mosaic. To create a contemporary look, you could assemble pieces in a less-uniform pattern, using random selections of glass or rounded glass pebbles for a colorful addition to your design.

Whether you will be finishing a large or small area, tile's color and design possibilities are vast and exciting. Tile can be the defining decorative element in a design, and it is frequently what leaves the most memorable impression of a kitchen or bath.

TOP: Orange glass tile enhances the entertaining mood of this beverage center.
BOTTOM: The varied tones of pebble tiles offer opportunities to create pattern.
OPPOSITE: A red tile backsplash warms up a stainless-steel-appointed kitchen.

precious metals

shiny or matte, metal details add color and style to any kitchen or bath

always think of metal in the kitchen or bathroom as the "sparkle factor." Adding a bit of brass, chrome, copper, bronze, or nickel on hardware or fixtures can bring out the personality in your design, especially when it's coordinated with the rest of the colors and elements of the room. All of these metals are available in matte or polished finishes. A matte finish is especially popular today, but the sheen of a highly polished metal can reflect light beautifully—so don't sell it short. Some metals—particularly cop-

per and bronze—can be given a rustic handmade look.

Stainless steel is a popular choice for kitchens, although you can find it in contemporary bathrooms. In general, stain-

BELOW: The polished finish inside this copper lav contrasts with the matte finish on the bowl's outside surface and the taps.
OPPOSITE: The warm copper accents add a finishing touch to this elegant faucet. Two-tone designs like this one work well with other metals in the room.

less steel has a modern look to it, but you can pair it well with transitional styles. Stainless steel usually has a satin finish, but it can be shiny, too. A shiny stainless-steel kitchen sink or appliance front is impractical, but on a countertop lav in the bath, the look is elegant—and less prone to damage.

You may have a little trouble trying to match all of the stainless steel in your kitchen. Stick with the same appliance manufacturer, and coordination will be easier. If you cannot find knobs or handles for doors in stainless steel, a brushed

OPPOSITE: Copper accents on this kitchen's range hood complement the room's warm tones in cream-color cabinetry. ABOVE: The faucet's matte finish has an understated look.

chrome or a satin-finish nickel is a good substitution.

In the bathroom, you could pair a polished stainless-steel lav with shiny chrome, nickel, glass, or crystal fittings for a glamorous uptown look. Pull the design together with matching towel bars and light fixtures.

Nickel is a slightly warmer, and thus a more traditional-looking, metal than chrome and stainless steel. In a satin or brushed finish, it can suit any decor. Polished nickel lends itself to a formal look. Nickel is a popular choice for hardware, which includes lighting fixtures, curtain rods, cabinet and door knobs and pulls, and faucets. Nickel can complement the color of any wood-stained or painted cabinet and any countertop.

To add extra warmth to a kitchen or

bath, you might consider earthy bronze or copper accents. Both have a classic appeal, as does the less-fashionable-at-the-moment brass. Newer to the market is rich bronze. A popular choice for faucets and light fixtures, such as sconces, it wears well—and the chocolate-brown color has a vintage Old World appeal. It looks especially attractive with medium- to light-color wood cabinets. Bronze comes in a matte or oiled (antique) finish. It adds warmth to a room with lots of stone surfaces or stainless-steel appliances. Its rustic quality makes it a natural to combine with concrete countertops and sinks, too.

Copper is a material that keeps changing over time. It may come lacquered to a high sheen or in a matte finish. Either way, copper can be smooth or hammered. Even the lacquered finish will wear, and the copper will mellow to a deep, rich brown patina—but that aged look is what most lovers of copper find so desirable. However, you can lessen the process by periodically applying wax to the copper surface, and you can repolish

TOP: The nickel leg on this claw foot tub adds glamour to the vintage design.
BOTTOM: A toilet handle in a satin-chrome finish coordinates with the rest of the hardware in the bathroom.
OPPOSITE: Stainless-steel cabinet pulls were inspired by the refrigerator.

it to restore the metal's shiny look, too.

Copper is a handsome choice for a sink or as an accent in tile, plumbing fittings, or hardware. Its reddish-orange-brown color is a warm counterpoint to cool colors and, in its deeper tones, coordinates well with brown, tan, and orange palettes. In addition, copper is a natural antibacterial, making it a healthy choice in a food-preparation area.

If you're looking for inspiration for choosing a metal, look at jewelry trends. Today, mixing metals or combining metal with another material is a fashionable option, especially with regard to cabinet hardware. When you're shopping for a faucet, you'll find numerous two-tone designs that combine cool chrome or nickel with warm brass, for example. You'll also see some designs that mix matte and polished finishes. The same goes for mixing stainless-steel appliances with another metal, such as bronze or nickel, in the kitchen. Let the room's overall style be your guide. Just don't mix too many looks or finishes in one place. Remember to consider the color of the metal as part of your overall scheme, coordinating it with tile, stone surfaces, and even the paint.

ABOVE: A metal-tile backsplash picks up the tones in this kitchen's granite countertop. The tile's satin finish adds gleam without glare and camouflages splatters.

Part 2

● ● ● ● ● ● ● ● ● ● ● ●

selecting your
STYLE

summer whites

a clean, light approach to creating a pristine palette in the kitchen and bath

white carrera marble

With a contemporary look, a clean white marble adds elegance to any bathroom. Here it is an understated and elegant choice for this countertop. A mid-tone wood accent keeps it from appearing cold.

lavender

A carefree hue to add to any all-white environment, lavender could be introduced in the room above as a cool accent color in towels and toiletries.

summer green

Pale green with a hint of yellow is another possible accent color for the all-white scheme, opposite. In this bathroom, it would be the perfect nature-inspired complement to the simple design.

spring yellow

Spring yellow would pick up the warm tones in this kitchen's creamy-white cabinetry, the tan and brown swirls in the granite countertop, and the deep honey-hue in the wood floor.

dutch blue

Dutch blue is a traditional color that would be an ideal accent for a formal white kitchen. In the one above, the color would provide a pleasant counterbalance to the room's warm tones.

taupe tile

This neutral color, a grayish tan, is always elegant when it's paired with crisp white. If you want to keep the look light with white cabinets and fixtures, a touch of taupe will accent it nicely.

smoky gray tile

Pairing this color with taupe and white tiles provides an opportunity to create a subtle pattern on the floor and around the mirror that keeps the all-white look from appearing stark.

orange glow
This white bathroom has playful notes provided by colorful, small glass accent tiles and matching glass knobs. Orange, in particular, denotes a youthful, happy mood.

pool-water blue
A soft touch, the towel's pool-water blue color is so feathery light that it never detracts from the almost all-white focus of the room's design.

colonial blue

This medium-tone gray-blue countertop pairs beautifully
with snowy-white bathroom cabinetry. Chrome faucets and
accessories enhance the cool palette.

slate blue

Strong gray-blue slate floor tile grounds the room.
A pretty print fabric on the bench bridges the dark and light
blue hues and enlivens the room with some pattern.

stainless steel

Stainless steel reflects the clean white lines of an
understated palette. A wood floor, opposite, prevents
the look from seeming too severe.

copper

Copper accents, provided by the cookware on the range top
opposite, offer another way to subtly add warmth without
introducing another paint color to the room.

fresh teal

This pale green-blue is a pretty accent for the kitchen above.
On the backsplash in the form of glass tile, it would look luminous
paired with under-cabinet lighting and the metal countertop.

cream yellow
This delicate color could bring together the warm tones
of the different woods in this kitchen. If you don't want to refinish
any surfaces, use towels or dishes to introduce the hue.

lime green
Add a splash of whimsy with this highly spirited color.
Look at the glass vase on the island to see how much life
just a dollop of this bright hue brings to the design.

earthy wood
A butcher-block countertop, wood furniture, baskets,
and matchstick blinds add perceptible warmth to this
large stark-white kitchen.

pale lavender
The pastel wall color adds an element of contrast to the white trim and cabinets in the cheerful kitchen, and it harmonizes with the coral red accents.

coral red
Used sparingly, this softer version of red is remarkable in its fresh, country-like appeal. It's uplifting and never overwhelming as an accent here.

bright yellow
Bright and upbeat, little bits of bright yellow catch your eye. Used only as an occasional accent in flowers or pottery, it has a playful effect.

cottage blue

Nothing looks more like summer than a pairing of deep blue and porcelain white. Accent it with wrought-iron, above, or polished-chrome hardware, opposite.

pale yellow

If the combination is too cool, you could warm it with a slight amount of pale yellow. Keep it subtle, especially if the wall or floor treatment is strong.

black and white and ...

*a palette that is
both classic and cheerful*

warm yellow

In towels or accessories, warm yellow would pick up
the tones of polished-brass hardware and provide just the
right amount of visual relief against the bold floor above.

spicy red

Spicy red looks dramatic paired with black and white. The color
plays off the whimsy of the harlequin pattern used to arrange the
marble tiles opposite.

coffee 'n' cream
A black-and-white marble floor underscores the formality of this handsome wood-paneled bathroom. To keep the look understated, accessorize with a subtle warm tone.

rich green
The depth of this shade of green would add the perfect contrast to the white tiles and fixtures. Green is always outstanding paired with natural wood.

slate gray

Slate gray is a sophisticared color choice for this countertop. It softens and complements the strong pattern on the floor and coordinates with the stainless-steel appliances and hardware.

winter gray-green

A classic, this gray-green would be a good choice as an accent color. Like the slate gray, it is soft but introduces a fresh color into the kitchen.

periwinkle blue
Periwinkle is a playful shade of blue. As an accent in a
black-and-white scheme, above and opposite, it looks fresh and
summery. Use a pale tone or a richer, full-bodied version.

distinctive gold
Gold can hold its own against a striking black-and-white
background. Try introducing it with two-tone hardware,
such as brass and chrome faucets.

cinnamon

With a spicy contemporary feel, cinnamon brown brings an earthy quality to these two kitchens, opposite and above, as an accent color in art and pottery.

earthy taupe

This soft version of taupe is a comfortable background color for the kitchen opposite. It is an elegant partner for the white cabinets and black countertop.

marble blue
Tying in with the gray streaks in the marble countertop,
a light blue accent is a gentle approach to adding color to
a room with a strong pattern, such as stripes, above.

charcoal gray
Another way to soften the black-and-white design is with
a dusty shade of charcoal gray. This lighter version of black
is both elegant and understated.

honey yellow

Even a small touch of honey yellow can go a long way in a black-and-white room. First, it warms a room with lots of cool white surfaces, and then it brightens the black.

Mexican red

A robust color for a strong design, this Mexican red accent pops in an otherwise colorless room. Use it sparingly; the strength of this color allows it to take center stage in a design.

white carrera marble
This beautiful stone has light gray veining that provides a subtle pattern. On the countertop and floor above, it contrasts elegantly with the room's dark vanity cabinet.

apple green
Apple green is such a pretty color. When it's used in a room with formal appointments or dark, somewhat masculine colors, it can create a pleasing balance of opposites.

pure and simple

easygoing and honest design for your home

slate gray

A soft neutral color is often a smart choice for a tile countertop and backsplash. Unassuming slate gray lets the colorful linoleum floor above make the room's design statement.

pale rust

A pretty color paired with cream-color cabinets, pale rust adds a warm accent to the cool minty green floor. It's always important to balance strong colors.

royal blue

In a small bathroom with a strong wall color, opposite, use accents sparingly. Here, all that's needed is a tiny pop of color from the royal blue hand towel.

details

A yellow breakfast nook is a cheerful place to start the day. With contrasting white-painted built-in banquettes topped with green cushions, the small space is as pretty as it is comfortable. Practical blinds can be adjusted to filter the sun.

sunshine yellow

You could introduce this delicate color to tie together the white woodwork and the bright yellow walls above. Pick it up in table linens or in a printed fabric that might be used for curtains.

willow green

Softer than bright Kelly green and with a more vintage feel to it, this color is the perfect choice for the banquette cushions. It's just right with the bright yellow walls.

oak honey spice

The warm tones of the wood table and chairs opposite inspired the yellow walls. Notice the checkered wood floor, too, which alternates a mid-tone with a deep-tone stain.

coffee 'n' cream
An earthy accent color in this bright blue-green room, coffee n' cream makes the large space feel cozier, especially because it's used on the floor.

rich green
Rich green has depth and sincerity. Inspired by the color of the plant's leaves, it would be a stylish choice for towels or for matting framed prints.

light teal

A versatile accent color, light teal allows the room to be either bright and playful or restrained and refined. Pale teal and delicate rose is a classic combination.

smokey taupe

Smokey taupe, an earthy gray hue, is a neutral that is harmonious with practically any palette. Here, it introduces a slightly stronger color to the overall pastel scheme.

details

Rich taupe-color walls look elegant in this understated bathroom. Taupe picks up the gray tones in the marble yet warms the overall scheme, which might otherwise appear too cool. Keeping the color palette simple is the key to this room's sophistication.

carrera marble

Traditional and elegant is the best way to describe this exquisite marble. The beauty of this natural stone is its veins of soft grays and, sometimes, creamy tans.

pool-water blue

Sweet and delicate, pool-water blue could add a refreshing, slightly more casual note to the all-neutral color palette and high-end design.

chocolate brown

Few colors can provide depth and warmth like a stunning rich version of brown. In a room with an understated palette, chocolate brown enhances the sense of luxury.

cream

Creamy and smooth, this quiet color brings together the stronger hues in the room, above. For a harmonious overall scheme, balance light and dark colors.

sunlit orange

Somewhere between yellow and pure orange is this beautiful color. It's outstanding against a neutral backdrop. You can use it sparingly—even the smallest dollop makes a big impact.

oak brown

A saturated dark brown color with a rich finish can be striking, whether it's a stained wood, paint, natural stone, tile, or laminate. Above, it grounds the room; opposite, it accents.

salmon peach
As a most delicate accent color, it stands out against the bold wall color above. Because the white surfaces are reflective, they pick up a touch of the color from the bath mat and towels.

ocean blue
A beautiful brighter blue adds a dainty quality to the unique folding screen. This decorative element has become an exciting focal point against the room's simple color palette.

details

A simple palette creates romantic ambiance in the bath and dressing room. What makes this room special is the blend of blues and subtle salmon peach, all brought together in a beautiful folding screen. It is visually pleasing and useful at the same time.

buttery cream

A warm color intended to soften the bright white paneling and bathroom fixtures can be seen on the upholstered bench seat. It also adds to the old-fashioned charm of the room.

blue-gray

This rich wall color looks outstanding in a large room with all-white fixtures. The white wainscot keeps the dark walls from overwhelming the space.

details

Update an older room with trendy accent colors. Here, a simple palette allows the accent hues to make an updated style statement. Use all three, or rotate colors with towels or small decorative objects when you're in the mood for a change.

avocado green

With a splash of retro-'70s style, this goldish green is the unexpected touch in this neutral color scheme. It has a light-hearted look and can be versatile.

coppery rust

Coppery rust is made for this color scheme. While it has an earthy quality, it also has enough spice to catch your eye, especially as an accent in a colorful rug or linens.

rich blue

Rich blue is the exact opposite of coppery rust on the color wheel—and opposites attract. But you can pair this strong hue with the avocado green, too.

warm and inviting

adding a cozy feeling to your kitchen and bath

pumpkin

Light-hearted pumpkin adds an easy-going accent to this earth colors-inspired kitchen. It especially picks up on the cabinet's wood tones.

honey

A beautiful hue for wood cabinets and floors, this mid-tone is rich but never overbearing. The stain shows off the wood's fine grain and texture against the muted hue of the pale olive-color walls.

black granite

The most dynamic color for a stone countertop is black. This black granite has flecks of brown that brings a subtle pattern into the room and picks up the warm tones used elsewhere.

ecru
Because the cabinetry and countertops in both rooms are strong, this mellow neutral is a good choice for the painted trimwork, above, and the tile backsplash, opposite.

warm yellow
A cabinet that has been painted warm yellow, opposite, is in striking contrast with the brick red walls. The color makes the cabinet look as though it's a freestanding piece of furniture.

rich green granite
In a room comfortable with strong hues this powerful color of granite fits right into the overall design. It offers an alternative to a black granite countertop.

Old World green

This soft, earthy green is reminiscent of a sun-drenched grove somewhere in Italy or southern France. It would be a beautiful accent in this kitchen.

country red

This irresistible shade of red attracts your eye as you enter the room. Against the warm creams and browns, it enhances the Old World flavor of the room's design.

details

This remarkable room has an elaborate design.
What makes it so inviting is that all of the patterns
and colors work beautifully together.

light brown

Light brown accents in the diagonal tile surrounding
the cooktop allude to shadings in the island's stone countertop
and helps to pull together the kitchen's color scheme.

walnut brown

Much of the cabinetry and trim in this room have
been stained deep walnut brown—another allusion to
the design's southern European theme.

silvery lavender
A softer gray with the slightest hint of lavender would be a pretty pastel accent color against this stone backdrop, tying together the white fixtures and the subtle variations in the stone.

walnut brown
In a bathroom with a lot of light tile, dark-stained wood cabinetry looks outstanding. In this room, a thin glaze tinted a slightly darker color than the stain adds character.

cinnamon red

This strong color adds personality in a room with lots of light wood cabinetry and neutral floor tile. If you want to sample this color before painting, do it with one or two decorative objects.

light Tuscan brown

A lighter stain color will keep a bathroom or kitchen with lots of cabinetry from overwhelming the space. Here, a light Tuscan brown is warm and versatile.

chestnut brown

A glaze added over this room's cream-color cabinet shows off all of the details on the painted vanity, makes it look like a fine antique, and echoes the aged finish on the wall.

light cool blue

Against the creams and browns, a breezy light blue would be a cheerful note in this serious room. Use it sparingly for a subtle note of color.

rust-brown stone

Although the stone top on this vanity is light granite, a deeper, more patterned slab could be the right alternative. Something with swirls of dark and mid-tones would add drama.

details

Earth tones and wood cabinets put a retro contemporary spin on this kitchen. Lots of sunlight, a white speckled backsplash, and a neutral color on the floor help to keep the mood lively and upbeat.

speckled stone

A light engineered-stone backsplash has an upbeat look. When it is brightly lit, the lighter surface is able to complement any color cabinetry or wall.

sunny yellow

A cheerful splash of color would fit right into this earth-tone scheme. Bright and animated, sunny yellow suggests an easygoing mood.

sky blue

The clean light in this room, thanks to expansive windows, would welcome beautiful sky blue as an accent color. Try it with pottery or serving pieces.

moss green

A stunning example of a color-tinted wood stain, the moss green above left has the right amount of earthiness to make it compatible with other natural hues in the room's palette.

burnt orange

Dazzling with dark cabinet colors, burnt orange adds energy to the room above right. Here, it is achieved with lighting, but you could bring it into the room with a glass-tile backsplash.

soft gray

This understated color is the perfect example of how
to use a soft accent color. In this case, it is a subtle
backdrop to the strong hues in the room.

dark woodsy brown

In stunning contrast to the soft gray floor, dark woodsy brown
stain on the island helps to make the cabinet a focal point in this
kitchen. It picks up on some of the wall's stone colors, as well.

subtle sand

The subtle sand hue of the floor and backsplash tile serves as a neutral backdrop for the saturated tone of the wood and the deep green wall color.

rich oak

The dramatic Arts and Crafts-style cabinetry sets the design motif for this room. The rich oak stain of the wood supports that theme. Additional furnishings complement the scheme.

details

This remarkable period-style kitchen is comfortable for
family time and entertaining. The rich, warm tones, especially that
of the cabinetry, make the room inviting.

warm gold

This luminous accent color fits right in with the rich browns
of the wood. Used as a punch color in the stained-glass window
and in the enameled cookware, it seems to glow.

gray stone

An understated countertop color in this spacious kitchen
allows the striking woodwork to get most of the attention, but
the variations in the stone lend their own subtle glamour.

tan
A tile design made up of coordinated neutral stone colors can be elegant. Done in contrasting pale and richer tans, the tile above is the focal point in the room.

light beige
A pale wall color against the strong tile patterns is tasteful. Mellow and light, the less-saturated color never distracts from the room's dramatic use of tile.

dusty green
A mellow dusty green blends naturally with dramatic stone and tile. Some of the same green can be found in the area rug opposite, which inspired the wall color.

bone white

Bone-white trim is a little warmer than a stark porcelain white, above. When you're pairing warm and cool whites, always use the warm version on the wall.

terra-cotta

This rusty terra-cotta color is just what is needed to make the room above less austere. It's also a tasteful bridge between the dark floor and white fixtures.

dark multicolor stone

A dark multicolor stone color for the floor would be elegant and rich. You can create it with stone tile or with ceramic tile that has the look and texture of stone.

carved
in stone

*adding richness
with the natural beauty
of stone*

pistachio green

This light green is compatible with an understated earth-tone color scheme. It would add a refreshing accent to the nature-inspired space opposite.

sienna brown

A striking accent for a room with lots of tan-color stone, sienna brown has an earthy clay quality to it. It is introduced here conservatively with towels (opposite).

cocoa

Cocoa, a luscious brown, brings out the deeper colors in natural wood. This strong hue would stand out beautifully against this restrained palette.

lilac

This delicate light purple adds a spark of romance to a room.
A lighthearted color, it is perfectly at home above in the bowl and
flowers. For a dash more of it, bring in lilac-colored candles.

white carrera marble

The satiny white of polished white marble calls attention
to the silvery veins in the stone. Combined with the
lilac accents, the look is luxurious.

evening blue

Drawing from the tender grays and blues in the stone
that surrounds the tub above, this rich color would look
cool and classic as an accent.

multicolor stone

In this quiet room with a subdued color scheme,
rich variegated stone is an important element. Look
for colors within the stone for accents and accessories.

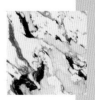

rusty black stone

Who says all the countertops have to match?
A dramatic black granite with rust-color swirls is
just enough for a small snack counter, above.

rusty brown stone

The rest of the kitchen island is topped with a
similar but slightly less showy granite. Nonetheless,
the two stones coordinate beautifully here.

brilliant yellow

In the elaborate kitchen opposite, you can see how brilliant yellow
is just the right accent. The cheerful color adds a touch of
informality to this room's formal features.

pistachio green
This pretty accent color would look fresh against the powerful slate stone here. In fact, it would soften the look of the tiles and make the bathroom cheerier.

rustic slate
This magnificent stone may feature blues, browns, grays, greens, and even black—sometimes in one large tile! Pick out one or two of these colors for other features in the room.

royal blue

In a room that has a narrow range of brown tones, above, a little bit of unexpected color is welcome. A tad of royal blue in a vase or a towel is an excellent way to introduce it.

taupe granite

In a bathroom with several different surfaces, a fine, smooth stone can bring the look together. Understated, an earthy and mellow color creates the perfect ambiance.

details

What is striking about this room is that the color cues all come from the natural elements—the slate tile on the backsplash and the wood cabinets, especially. Remember, "natural" doesn't mean colorless—there are many shades and tones in nature.

marigold

To bring out the color variation in the natural stone and the warmth of the wood cabinets, try adding golden marigold to the scheme.

honey wood

The warmest color you can stain wood cabinets is honey. In this kitchen, it looks just right because its warmth is balanced by the cool tones in the slate tile.

cool slate

A range of blues, gray-greens, and deeper golds provides a varied palette for pulling out colors that can be elsewhere in the kitchen, such as the chair cushion's fabric.

bright gold
Warmer than bright yellow, this color would pick up
the golden tones of the woods in both kitchens,
above and opposite, without looking garish.

slate
Predominantly brown slate on the kitchen floors features
an array of shades, from intensely chocolate to orange-brown.
These hues play off the wood grains nicely.

black galaxy granite
Darkest black granite is as posh as it comes. It brings a
dynamic sense of style to these two kitchens, which are both
dominated by wood.

dusty teal

Dusty teal can bring out the highlights in richly colored slate, especially if the stone has lots of gray, gray-green, and black tones. For the best result, use it sparingly as an accent.

honey wood cabinetry

Because the dark tones that are in the slate tile predominate, the lighter honey color of the cabinet acts as an accent in the room above.

taupe granite

Mixing stones is perfectly acceptable if you coordinate colors. This taupe granite has a tight pattern that works well as a tub deck with a slate-tile surround and floor, opposite.

a softer approach

gentle color schemes for kitchens and baths

true wheat

To add a cozy touch to such a pure and simple design, introduce a warm color on an accent piece. A good example is the true wheat rug, which is still delicate in tone.

plum

This would be an interesting complementary hue for the bathroom above if you wanted to add one punch color. Rich and saturated, use plum in small doses.

This bathroom has the qualities of a charming vintage design that has been freshened with a contemporary upbeat palette. The sweet light green walls and crisp white fixtures make the space pleasant in every way. A good tip: select delicate accents so as not to overshadow the overall scheme of soft color.

lavender
Adding a light purple to this room would be delightful and a bit whimsical. Sometimes a playful little touch of color can add a whole lot of charm!

black-brown
This intensely dark floor anchors the lighter palette in the room. A high contrast against the bright white painted wood and fixtures, it grounds the design.

floral pink
Floral pink is sweet and delicate, so it's a good choice for accenting a room with a soft wall color. When it's very pale, pink can act as a neutral. Try it out with fresh flowers.

cloudy blue
This dusty shade of blue is another option for a pastel room. Keep to a similar value or intensity of the wall color to maintain the understated appeal of the room.

oatmeal

A soft neutral will tone down a room that gets strong natural
light. As the color chosen for the window treatment and
the rug above, it keeps the white surfaces from reflecting glare.

mottled gray-taupe stone

If you wanted to add a stone surface to this room, a granite
with lots of gray and taupe tones would be a good choice.
The stone and its cool hues would complement the wall color.

tomato red

A kitchen with creamy white and pale yellow surfaces, above, can handle a zesty accent color like tomato red. Small dabs of it add just the right amount of energy to the scheme.

multicolor stone

This kitchen's multicolor granite countertops provide a starting point for choosing other colors for the room. The vermillion shadings in the stone suggest red accents, for example.

classic black

Black grounds a room. For example, in the kitchen opposite, a black-painted worktable anchors the food-prep area. Other small black touches, such as the accent tiles, pull the look together.

delightful pink
Sweet and innocent, this casual shade of pink would be
versatile paired with the light yellow-green in this breakfast
area. The inspiration? The pretty spring tulips.

periwinkle blue
Another suggestion would be the slightly purple-blue called
periwinkle. It has a whimsical look, so you might want
to use it as table linens or dishes for a celebration.

cloud white

Among a rich field of multicolor tile, small white ones
add a light-hearted quality to the backsplash. Their slightly
blue cast picks up the shades of gray tile in the design.

warm mid-tone wood

A warm mid-tone stain used on the cabinets keeps this modern
room warm and inviting. Other warm colors in the room include
those in the upholstery and the pendant light fixtures.

melon orange

In these two bright white kitchens, melon orange looks lighthearted and playful. Use it for table linens and dishes. Remember, orange stimulates the appetite.

brown-red granite

You might want to warm an all-white scheme with a countertop that has shades of browns and earthy red. Against the painted cabinets, this counter stone really shines.

off-white wood

Cream-color neutral cabinets allow you to decorate and accent with any number of hues. If your palette is more cool, forgo the cream and choose arctic white.

details

In a room without a lot of natural light, painted cabinetry is a great option. If you spend a lot of time in your kitchen and you are more comfortable in a bright space, consider painting the cabinets a soft, light color. It could create the mood you are seeking.

sunflower yellow

Look at how this luminous color draws your eye to the flowers on the hutch opposite. If you want to brighten the mood in a room with dark corners, this color will do it.

slate blue

A beautiful rich color with an antique feel to it, this subdued blue is a lovely backdrop for warm white cabinetry in a traditional or period-style room.

creamy white

This warm shade of white pairs beautifully with cool slate blue. Besides using it for cabinetry, you could pick it up in tile or by painting the trimwork in the room with it.

chestnut brown

Adding a rich dark brown to a cool color scheme softens the room's appearance. Here, it's used as a stain for the wood cabinets, but you could add it with towels.

chrome

The metals in your kitchen or bath should be considered in your scheme. Chrome has a cool silver look to it, making it a natural choice for both of these icy blue rooms.

metal and glass

add polish with materials that sparkle

bronze

With shiny reflective wall treatments, such as the bamboo effect created with tile above, bronze would add an exotic touch. Look for it in faucets and lavs.

gold

In a room with cool stone underfoot and pristine white porcelain fixtures, take a color cue from a warm metal, such as the matte-gold mirror frame opposite, to inspire a wall color.

blue-gray
Whether the gray has hints of blue or blue-purple, this color looks spectacular in a contemporary room with chrome, silver, or stainless-steel surfaces and hardware.

chrome
Polished or matte finished, chrome is always a popular choice for kitchen and bath hardware. But it is particularly compatible with white fixtures and gray or white stone.

stainless steel

For appliances, countertops, tile, and hardware, stainless steel is popular today. You can see that it makes a big design statement in both of these kitchens, opposite and above.

sunny yellow

A solid-surface countertop in warm sunny yellow, above, is an interesting and unexpected choice to pair with the cool stainless-steel tiles on the backsplash. Opposites attract!

multicolor slate

With varied grays, golds, and browns, slate floor tile brings a rustic warmth to the modern design opposite. It counterbalances the kitchen's stainless-steel elements, too.

creamy yellow
Bringing out the highlights in the wood, a creamy
yellow would be a pleasing color in the setting above.
Pick it up in towels or pottery.

delicate sky blue
This soft color would complement the yellow tones
of the wood used for the vanity. Delicate colors are good
choices for rooms with lots of reflective glass.

golden wood
Light yet warm, this color will draw you into a room,
especially one that is large and airy. It's the perfect choice
to balance the cool surfaces.

gray-green

The gray-green color in this bathroom draws attention
to the deeper values in the stripes of metallic paint. The
bathroom's chrome fittings pull the design together.

adobe clay

Bringing an earthy accent into this room would add
a cozier feel to the palette. Adobe clay is a good choice
for towels, a rug, or even pottery.

silver

A touch of silver, perhaps in a mirror frame, can accentuate the
metallic stripes. Sometimes even the most understated reflective
accents can be the most pleasing.

slate gray
Finding a stone color to coordinate with the steel or chrome in a kitchen is usually easy, especially in the case of slate, which has a lot of gray in its coloration.

cobalt blue
A cobalt blue glass pendant brings a colorful surprise into this scheme. Use an unexpected touch of strong color for an interesting twist in an all-neutral room.

copper

Copper pot accents blend beautifully into this country-style kitchen, picking up the warm highlights in the wood floor and adding to the richness of the pumpkin-painted paneled wall.

cream

Painted cream-color cabinetry is a pleasant bridge between the cool stainless-steel appliances and the warm copper and pumpkin accents in this room.

royal navy blue
The dramatic dark blue tile on the backsplash helps to make the cooking area a focal point in the design by providing a dramatic backdrop for the sleek stainless-steel hood and range.

warm honey
Wood cabinetry finished with a warm honey-tinted stain stands out beautifully against the shiny metal, blue, gray, and rich black in this contemporary kitchen.

black
Dynamic and elegant, black accents would be stunning against the dramatically lit backsplash and rich cabinet color in the kitchen above.

garnet
Sleek and irresistible, these cabinets feature a garnet-tinted stain that shows off the beautiful graining in the wood. This dark red-brown complements the cool steel hardware.

deep periwinkle

Sharing blue and purple, this color adds a fun accent to the design above. Just a hint, in the glass vase and towel, is enough to add extra personality.

multicolor brown stone

In a room with lots of metal (appliances and the island cabinet, here), a stone countertop can have a lively, warm pattern. In this case, the stone reveals lots of gold and brown tones.

apple green

Playful apple green would capture the brightest reflections
in either of these rooms. If you want to add a youthful touch,
this is the color that can do it.

wild plum

Deep wild plum, on the other hand, is mature. It adds
depth to the room opposite. A combination of a strong color
and metallic and glass surfaces always looks dramatic.

chrome

The beauty of this silver-like metal is that it can be
an accent or the focus of the room. A polished finished
will reflect the other colors.

sweet salmon

A delicate color, sweet salmon would add a subtle note
to the daring room opposite. If you want a touch of hue
that won't detract from a unique look, choose a soft color.

jet black

A jet black stone with subtle veining is a good choice
to top the brushed-metal vanity above. The stone has just enough
crystallizations to gleam when the light hits it.

rich and luxurious

create elegance with sumptuous color

taupe

As a color for trimwork and decorative elements, taupe could bring out the mellow tones of the stone floor above. You can use this color to pull together mutiple colors in a stone.

midnight green

With a contemporary look to it, deep midnight green can be striking against a neutral palette, as evidenced in the stained glass shown opposite.

butterscotch stone

The warm golden brown shadings in some marbles and granites let them coordinate beautifully with natural colors, such as the midnight green and taupe.

slate gray

A fabulous color paired with creams, this slate gray creates an elegant contrast. Neutral with the slightest hint of blue, this cool color grounds the room above.

creamy white

Adding a vintage feeling to standard bright white, this cozy color is magnificent on cabinetry and flooring. More mellow than its crisp version, creamy white is perfect in a traditional room.

gauzy gray

Applied to light painted surfaces, a glaze with a gauzy gray tint can make cabinets and islands look like time-honored antiques. Pair this color with slate gray or taupe features in the room.

golden brown leather

A wonderful, warm color, this plush tint looks rich
and buttery soft. Introduce it in the bath as an accent color
in candles, pottery, glass, or linens.

cranberry red

Cranberry red can be an eye-catching note in either of these
rooms. If you want to maintain the low-key color scheme, try it in
a small patterned rug or as a color for matting artwork.

rich teak

Teak is a practical and handsome choice for wood surfaces in a
bathroom. This rich color is elegant, yet appealing, even in a
comtemporary room.

details

Glowing in pale yellow, the cabinetry in this elaborate kitchen is stunning. With the texture of the stone countertop, luxurious chandeliers, and exquisite details, the look is top of the line.

rich purple

This marvelous purple is a perfect complementary color against the strong yellows. Used sparingly for flowers or glassware it could be exceptional in this setting.

gold

This room and it's buttery yellow palette reflects the light of the sun all day. Carry the yellows to the metal in the form of brass, or extend it to gold accents on dinnerware.

golden peach stone

Freckled with golden peach hues, the kitchen's granite countertop continues the warm palette. The stone's pattern adds more interest and texture, as well.

details

With exotic colors, this bathroom has a unique, bohemian style. The saturated hues, along with the weathered look applied to the walls, make this room unique and luxurious.

weathered gray
The textured weathered gray on the upper portion of the wall and ceiling draws attention to the architecture. Because it's lighter than the rest of the wall color, it "lifts" the height of the room.

caramel
Caramel could be used to lighten the tone of the decor. Warm and friendly, it would add an approachable, less mysterious look to the overall design.

chestnut brown
This deep brown, whether it is applied as a stain to wood or painted on a surface to appear like wood, adds an earthy warmth. Here, it's handsome on trimwork and the door.

honey gold
Bright and warm, the luxurious wall color was inspired
by the golden tones in the room's marble tile floor. It is also used
as an accent color in the rug and the candles.

black-green marble
Truly glamorous, this extravagant bathroom shows off the faux
black-green marble on the columns and trimwork by contrasting
it with the golden tones in the space.

jet black

Juxtaposed with eleborate gold fittings and other decorative gold-tone items, the jet black lav looks first class. This is always an elegant combination.

antique gold

This room has polish thanks to antique gold finishes that have been used lavishly. The color is a standout particularly with the green walls and black accents.

vintage charm

creating a gracious and time-honored decor

rich lilac

This color would be charming in the ornate setting opposite. It could also be a light-hearted contrast to the yellow toile wallcovering in the powder room above.

bronze

A rubbed-bronze finish on hardware suggests age. A fine example is on the vanity's antiqued legs, the mirror frame, and the wall-mounted fittings of the room opposite.

rose
Rose has a sweet, old-fashioned charm. In this bathroom with reproduction fixtures, it would be an appealing accent color to the light green on the wall.

lavender
Lavender is sweetness—with a twist. This spunky color can feel quaint and Victorian or whimsical and even a little wild. It all depends on the style of the room.

natural pine
The light wood floor adds a fresh, informal note to the bathroom. A clear, nonyellowing polyurethane was applied to the pine to keep the look and color natural.

sage green
An old-fashioned color with new appeal is subtle
sage green. It would add to the rich woods and golds in
the room above and underscore the period appeal.

aubergine
This sophisticated color is full of charm. It suggests
strength and softness at the same time. At its most saturated,
it can allude to the most dramatic Victorian splendor.

cocoa brown
In this grand bathroom, with its dark cabinetry and leather
seating, luscious brown would provide a rich accent. It would be
a handsome choice for velvety towels, too.

light gold
Light gold brings together all of the golden tones in
the woods in both of these kitchens, above and opposite.
Pick it up in an accent tile, fabrics, or pottery.

vintage rose
A charming color like vintage rose is at home in any traditional-style
kitchen or bath. It's a soft accent that can be played up in linens, a
print fabric, or flowering houseplants.

true blue

A blue-and-white check floor makes a big statement in the kitchen opposite. It's not as formal looking as black and white, so it's perfect for a country or cottage decor.

rustic red

Inspired by old table linens, rustic red is another great color for a vintage kitchen. In the room above you can see how it pops on the floor and in the seat cushions.

stainless steel

A stainless-steel countertop, above, looks as suitable in this vintage design as it would in a modern setting. Its steely gray hue acts as a neutral color, so you can pair it with anything.

henna

In bathrooms with such earthy palettes, warm henna would be a welcome addition. Its extra touch of brightness can prevent browns and tans from looking somber.

truffle brown

The very dark stain looks magnificent on formal styles of cabinetry. In the Old World-inspired design shown opposite, the color is also picked up in the pleated-shade fabric.

satin nickel

Satin nickel looks a bit like a matte chrome, but it's warmer. It's an excellent choice for a kitchen or bath that is more traditional than modern.

rustic red

A bold accent such as rustic red would certainly stand out in either of these neutral schemes. But you must use it gingerly, or you could spoil the intended low-key design.

works of art

*accenting
kitchens and baths with
artistic touches*

details

The delicate painting on the walls of this bathroom is graceful and charming. Done in a subtle palette of colors, it shows that even quiet designs can look outstanding.

gray-green

A mellow accent in this peach-color room, gray-green has a soft, cooling effect on the warm overall palette. This color can be used for velvety soft pillows, towels, or artwork.

coral

A stronger color than the wall's faint peach, this rich accent would add depth to the scheme. By bringing a darker color into this delicate room, the bright white features would be outstanding.

gold

The gold tone of the polished-brass fittings pulls together all of the warmest colors in this room. It complements the pristine white fixtures and painted paneling.

details

The colors and themes of this decorative painting are captivating against the natural woods in this room. The motif makes this woodsy bathroom seem to be outdoors.

sky blue
Bringing the sky blue background into the rest of the room with soft towels adds a light and pleasing contrast against the warm wood tones of the vanity and paneling.

chocolate brown
Rich and sumptuous, this strong color would bring out the deeper wood tones in the room. Chocolate brown is intense enough to add depth to this light-hearted space.

metallic gold
Metallic gold is an accent color with pizzazz—and
appropriately glitzy for these glamorous designs.
Gold-tone faucets and hardware pull it together.

green
Feathery light, green brings out the rich colors in the wall murals.
Use this beautiful accent for the cozy towels or bring in lush,
leafy plants for natural color.

details

A cross between elegant and exotic, the murals in
these rooms create an ambiance of absolute luxury.
With painted palm trees and scenery, these
rooms are unparalleled in their design.

light taupe

As an earth tone, this neutral color complements all of the
cream and tan colors in these rooms. It's outstanding as an
accent in the floor's tile design, opposite.

off-white marble

With pale taupe veining, the marble on the floor in the bathroom
above looks luxurious but subtle. Keep stone patterns simple in a
room where there's lots of things going on in the decor.

blue-gray

This dusty blue-gray is a good-looking color against the classic black-and-white tile design. Selecting a softer wall color allows the artwork to be the focal point in the room.

black

When in doubt, go for black. This color is always a classic addition to any color scheme whether it's a large part of the design or just a small accent used to anchor various hues.

rich red

A velvety rich red accent could add a spark to this subdued color scheme. It would bring out the red tones in the wood. There is a precedent for it in the painting, too.

rich brown

A rich brown stain on the wood cabinet adds elegance to this contemporary design. Dark woods have a more formal, dressier appearance than light woods.

details

Overlapping motifs that incorporate grasses, fruits, and flowers comprise a delicately painted swag border near the top of the wall in this eat-in kitchen. There's also a trompe l'oeil cupboard with a "pottery collection."

wheat

This low-key wall color is perfect as a backdrop for the painted effects. It's the combination of this quiet color and the artful details that make this room personal and pretty.

sweet green

Brighter and more playful than wheat, this sweet green would draw out the other green colors in the paintings. As an accent, it's perfect for table linens or seat cushions.

dusty rose

Dusty rose, inspired by the flowers in the painted swag, is a color with vintage appeal. In this country-style room, it's an excellent accent on the chair cushions.

raisin

A warm reddish brown, raisin is a deep color that would pick up on tones in the room's wood furniture. It could be an alternative to the dusty rose or another accent color.

details

This small beach-inspired powder room features a whimsical hand-painted mural and a color palette that feels like a day at the shore.

dark denim blue

Picked up from the blue beach chairs in the mural, this accent color can be used in the form of towels or a window treatment. It helps to carry through the theme suggested by the ocean.

brandy brown

An oak floor with a brandy-brown stain enhances the natural feeling in this design. It's a tint that works perfectly in tandem with the sandy-color walls.

blue-gray

A simple polished-concrete counter that has been colored blue-gray works in harmony with the brushed-nickel finish on the faucet and other hardware.

details

Rich with mood and texture, these beautiful painted clouds and ocean will carry you away. To complete the picture, you'll need the right accent colors for everything from linens to metals.

royal blue

This color would add to the nautical theme. Some touches of it wouldn't darken the mood. Use it for hand towels or as a small detail in floor or wall tile.

white marble

Nothing looks fresher than blue and white. So it's easy to see why white marble would be a classic addition to a design inspired by the sea.

chrome

Adding reflective sparkle, shiny polished chrome is just the right cool touch for this blue room. Here, it's carried over from the faucets to the console sinks' legs to the mirror and the sconces.

a playful ambiance

*have fun with your
kitchen and bath colors*

tangerine
Strong tangerine-color walls make this room come alive.
A vibrant color scheme can put your family in a happy mood in
the morning.

mustard gold
Adding a spicy sink and counter color to this energetic scheme is
a bold choice. With an earthy flavor, this strong hue plays off the
tangerine walls and wood-stained cabinet drawers.

gold stone
A custom shower built with a gold-hue concrete completes
the picture. If you have trouble matching the color, look
for a similar surface made from engineered stone.

metallic gold

This eye-catching metallic gold-framed mirror wears the most
important color in the rich blue room opposite. The over-the-top
choice is radiant against this dark blue wall.

deep periwinkle

You may want to play it safe in the family bath, but feel free to get
a little daring with color in a powder room. Case in point, the room
above that pairs a moody wall color with an artful glass lav.

khaki

This light earthy color allows stronger colors to take center stage.
It's a good choice for fixtures, as well, because it is a neutral tone
that will coordinate with many other hues.

sweet pink

A darling color, sweet pink is quite unexpected in most kitchens. But in the room above it's one among several perky hues with a retro feel that were selected for the backsplash tile.

cambrian black

Together with the colorful backsplash, this rich Cambrian black granite looks outstanding. Tiny crystals within the stone add some sparkle to the surface.

jade

Selecting this bright jade green to paint the kitchen floor above was bold, but the color carries the day. White cabinets and counters let you choose accent colors with abandon.

light gold

Paired with the jade green floor—and the small blue-and-white check tile backsplash—it's a winning look for a playful country kitchen. In a large space, you can use several fun colors.

glowing yellow

In a kitchen with a predominantly green and blue palette, this luminous shade of yellow adds just the right punch as an accent in the tile backsplash.

Kelly green

A lighter version of the strong cabinet color, bright Kelly green is dominant in the backsplash. It holds its own in the multicolor backsplash.

royal blue

Dazzling rich royal blue adds depth to the kitchen's color scheme. In a room with several strong hues, this blue's intensity gives it the clout it needs to be seen.

lime green
This light-hearted yellowy green adds zing to the rest of
the color scheme in this kitchen. Use it as an accent or for
table linens when you want an extra splash of color.

sunlight yellow
This vibrant yellow adds sunshine to a cool color
palette like this one. If you're daring, select this hue
for a countertop, or for just a section of one.

playful purple
Spirited and bright, this color brings out the purple
tones in the perwinkle-blue walls. Try accenting with
purple in a piece of pottery or with fresh flowers.

details

Feathery light blue walls
have a youthful appeal.
With crisp white cabinets
and flooring, this kitchen's
ready for a variety of
whimsical color accents.

sunshine yellow

The perfect accent against the light blue kitchen, this
yellow seems to sing in this room. Use it sparingly as a window
treatment or for dishes.

light gray

Soft light gray is an alternate choice for flooring and cabinetry
in a room like this one. Amost a darker version of white, light gray
is perfect if you want to tone down brightness.

navy blue
A bold navy blue is a strong accent color for this
light color scheme. With white cabinets and a light wall
color, navy blue will stand on its own.

classic orange
As an alternative to yellow, classic orange is pure fun.
It could be an outstanding choice as a punch color for
textiles, such as towels, table linens, or curtains.

natural maple

Simple natural maple cabinets are a good choice here. Their understated elegance and quiet color allows the use of exuberant hues on other surfaces in the room.

apple green

Playing against the rich green backsplash and green speckled countertop, this tangy color is a whole lot of fun.
Use it as an accent color in decorative elements and glassware.

details

This kitchen's color scheme is truly one of a kind. With gutsy selections for the tile backsplash and bright countertop, it's personality plus! To pull off a look like this one, you have to love color and can't be afraid of using it.

aquamarine blue

A bright, slightly greenish blue, this color has retro appeal. It's happy days all over again in a kitchen with several accents or features done in aquamarine blue.

sunflower yellow

The happiest of colors, sunflower yellow is luminous and pure. With a palette this wild, use this bright color for small touches—towels, table linens, or of course, fresh flowers!

willow green

Both of these bathrooms feature floor-to-ceiling glass tiles
in various shades of mostly green and brown. This is the lightest
of the greens. Use it as an accent with linens.

aquamarine blue

In the room opposite, there are a few aquamarine tiles scattered
throughout the design. They lift the mood of the room and provide
a little relief from the almost all-green wall.

chrome

Chrome faucets and hardware add sparkle to both
of these designs. For extra glitz, you could bring in another
metallic accent with a lighting fixture.

lemon lime

In this playful kitchen, an animated color, such as
lemon lime, would be a welcome addition to the palette.
It's fun and cheerful. Add it with small accent pieces.

mineral blue

This color would bring a retro feeling into this kitchen.
Placing this hue against the strong dark periwinkle, black, and
white palette would be striking.

violet

An alternative to the wall color is soft violet, which appears in
periwinkle blue. This option would tone down the overall look of
the room if it's used on its own, allowing strong accents to pop.

sand

The quiet color of the stone tub surround and shower enhances the peaceful mood of the room. All the color drama comes from the saturated navy blue wall.

mint green

Adding a playful mint green accent would enliven the scheme. This color has a light-hearted feeling that would counterbalance the intensity of the wall color.

black

As a strong punch color, this classic hue would be elegant in small touches, such as towels, for example. Or accent with a few pieces of pottery made with a matte black finish.

olive lime

The walls in these powder rooms are wild, but it's OK to go a little crazy with color in a room where you won't spend a lot of time. Here's your chance to make a statement!

bronze

A handsome rubbed-bronze finish was selected for the above-counter lav and wall-mounted fittings above. It helps to reinforce the look of an old garden with gracefully aged vessels.

off-white

Choosing a light color for cabinetry allows you to add more playful accents to the other features. A red wall and island are standouts next to the off-white units.

cherry red

It's red and it's stunning in this room. If you want red walls, remember all versions are not the same. This one has a touch of blue in it. For something earthier, select a brick red.

cobalt

This is another strong color, so if you add it to this scheme, do it in small doses. For example, try a display of cobalt glassware in a glass cabinet, opposite.

avant-garde style

try a clean and ultramodern approach to design

merlot

An intense dark red-brown, merlot makes a bold statement on an accent wall in this open layout. The color choice pairs beautifully with the mostly light tones in the room.

butternut

The light butternut stain on the wood cabinetry enhances the contemporary look here. At the same time, it keeps the modern room from appearing cold.

polished black

Countertops of polished concrete bring a touch of formal elegance into this modern design. It complements the room's metallic and wood finishes.

sand

The sand-color tile in this spacious bathroom suggests the feeling of a beach. It brings together the all-neutral look that accentuates the style's simplicity.

water green

Cool and restful, pale water green would be a good color for a few accents here. The entire space would look brighter if this pretty pastel hue paired with the earth tones.

spice

Mellow and inviting, the mid-tone spice color that has been chosen for the wood paneling and tub surround makes this large space feel intimate and soothing.

slate gray
A quiet color, slate gray allows the other colors and textures in the room to be important. This simple soothing neutral creates the perfect backdrop for the ultramodern design.

fawn
The faint fawn stain on the vanity counterbalances the cool slate gray of the tile. By creating equilibrium between these two dominant elements, the colors bring harmony to the scheme.

lipstick red
A splash of loud color makes a big hit in an otherwise quiet room. If it feels too risky to use it on a permanent fixture, such as the sink here, try it with towels or flowers.

sweet butter

To tone down the bright colors in this room, try
sweet butter. Add this soft yellow hue with dishes or pottery to
make the room's color palette a tad warmer.

lime green

Youthful lime green is a daring choice for the upholstery in
this eating area, especially because there are so many reflective
surfaces, such as the white walls and glass.

cobalt

The choice of cobalt cabinets in a kitchen, opposite, that is made
of almost entirely concrete surfaces lightens the mood—even if
the color is strong.

rich avocado
A stronger version of the green on the wall,
rich avocado can add an attractive additional layer
of color to this nature-inspired room.

plum red
Contrasting with the light green on the walls, plum red
looks strong. It has the satisfying intensity of a traditional
burgundy, but it's slightly bluer.

walnut brown
Because this room is almost monochromatic, the color of the
wood has more visual weight. This nutty brown is carried from
the wood vanity to the mosaic glass wall tiles.

honey marigold
This color is rich. As an accent, it would coordinate beautifully with the luxurious wood cabinetry and flooring and all of the jet-black surfaces in the room above.

jet black
Modern design is usually considered more casual than traditional styles. But black appliances and black granite countertops lend an urbane look to this room.

feathery light blue

As a gentle accent color for this no-nonsense design, feathery light blue would make the kitchen above look less serious without adding a jarring contrasting color.

charcoal gray

Charcoal gray, as seen on the soapstone countertop and backsplash, looks sleek and modern in this fashion-forward room. This color coordinates well with stainless steel.

orange-rust
This orange-rust color jumps out in this bathroom comprising several shades of gray. In an all-neutral scheme, one lively accent color can dramatically change the room's personality.

pebble gray
The pebble-gray palette opposite was inspired by the "pebble" floor tiles. With just a slight hint of blue in the wall tiles, this cool color looks ultramodern.

dark walnut
The deep black-brown stain on the paneling opposite looks rich against the pebble-gray tile. It has some warm undertones that keep the scheme from appearing cold.

stainless steel

This metallic finish serves as a neutral accent color in the kitchen above. It pulls together all of the metal in the room, appearing on chair stools, light fixtures, and appliances.

cherry red

An animated color in any modern palette, playful cherry red "lifts" the deep grays, blacks, and browns in the kitchen opposite. This stylish color packs a punch.

dark slate gray

A deep neutral hue on the floor and countertops accentuates the colors in both of the rooms shown here. Dark slate gray is striking but softer than solid black.

brushed blue

A lighter version of the rich blue walls in both of these rooms is this medium-tone brushed blue. It could stand up to the darker version as an accent on a feature wall or in smaller touches.

stone tan

A neutral-color stone is the perfect balance for the dramatic blue wall opposite. It's earthy and warm, qualities that differ from the cool sophisticated blue.

honey wood

A warm wood stain like this honey complements the deep blue thanks to the golden tones in the color. It's a standout on the wall above and on the vanity opposite.

traditional design

try classic colors in your kitchen and bath

dusty rose
To make the room above a bit more feminine, add accents in dusty rose. Use it as a solid color for linens or find a printed rug that features this vintage rosy hue in its pattern.

natural light pine
A vanity cabinet with a clear stain stands out against dark bead-board paneling and trim in the bathroom on the opposite page. The lighter wood color updates the entire design of the room.

lemon yellow
Even the smallest amount of this crisp yellow is visually
pleasing in a room with lots of green. Look at how the bowl of
lemons (and limes) grabs your attention in the room opposite.

honey wood
This mellow tone is a good choice for a wood stain in
a traditional setting. You can see how much warmth it adds
to the antique tables featured in both of these rooms.

traditional green
Dynamic for kitchens, traditional green has a history as
a color preference for cabinets in period rooms. It suggests
the luscious bounty of a summer garden.

light tan
Delicate light tan would be a soothing accent color
in this boldly striped bathroom. On the pillows and wall art, the
color would coordinate beautifully with the general palette.

sky blue
Another delicious accent for a neutral palette of colors
would be the ever-pleasing sky blue. Luminous in a room with
calming earth tones, sky blue is like a breath of fresh air.

matte black
The bold black color of the built-ins in this handsome bathroom
adds elegance. To carry it further, add towels in the same color or
swap the chrome fittings for matte black ones.

vivid yellow

Vivid yellow would energize a neutral kitchen with lots of wood surfaces. Because it is so bright, you have to use it sparingly and in a space that doesn't get too sunny.

deep red

As traditional as apple pie, deep red makes the perfect statement in the room above. See how it pops on the teapot? Another easy way to add it is with tile.

maple spice

A rich maple spice stain is a warm mid tone that's perfect for a kitchen that draws on traditional architectural features to make its design statement.

brick red

Brick red on the countertop near the window adds another layer of Mediterranean spice to this kitchen. The earthy accent's inspiration came from a color in the window shade's fabric print.

olive green

Painting some of the cabinetry olive green enhances the flavor of the room's Old World look. This shade of green has lots of yellow in it, which makes it warm and cozy.

hazelnut

Natural stained-wood cabinets in a hazelnut color would tie together all of the other hues and themes in the room. Its deep warm tones are rich and inviting.

copper
Stunning metallic copper can look both high spirited
and high style. Catching the eye in pots and pans here,
it coordinates well with the stainless steel in the room.

jet black
A dynamic color for a kitchen is trendy jet black,
especially on cabinets or furniture. Here, it's
a great foil for the intense acid-green walls.

true gold

True gold is a toned-down version of yellow that never looks too bright in an area that gets lots of daylight, such as this dining bay. Use it with fancy napkins or a table runner.

burgundy

An ever-popular color, this dark red would be a sumptuous addition to the earthy palette here. In sharp contrast to the sage green and taupe, red would energize the area.

clay

Clay is an earthy combination of orange, brown, and red. As an accent in this kitchen, it would stand out against the slate blue cabinets because the two colors are almost complementary.

slate blue

This cool blue-gray has a folksy look to it that makes it a perfect choice for painted cabinets in a traditional or country-style kitchen. Here, the slate countertop brings out the gray tones.

butter yellow

The soft creamy look of butter yellow blends beautifully with the off-white cabinetry and trimwork in the sophisticated room opposite, and that of the cottage-style bath above.

sage green

The sage green ceiling is a unique application of a great color. In this tall formal space, a touch of color on the ceiling visually adjusts the scale of the space and helps to make it more cozy.

creamy off-white
A light color-cabinet has a refined and understated look. It also lets you chose from a greater array of colors for countertops, walls, and floors.

classic green
Classic green is a favorite of designers. It would look exceptional in these traditional-style rooms with creamy off-white because it picks up a tiny bit of the yellow tone in the neutral color.

resources

The following list of manufacturers and associations is meant to be a general guide to additional industry and product-related sources. It is not intended as a listing of products and manufacturers represented by the photographs in this book.

Armstrong World Industries
717-397-0611
www.armstrong.com
Manufactures flooring, ceiling, and cabinet products.

Benjamin Moore & Co.
800-344-0400
www.benjaminmoore.com
Manufactures paint, stains, and varnishes.

Brookhaven Cabinets, a div. of Wood-Mode
877-635-7500
www.wood-mode.com
Manufactures semicustom cabinetry.

Corian, a div. of DuPont
800-426-7426
www.corian.com
Manufactures solid-surfacing material.

Crossville, Inc.
931-484-2110
www.crossvilleinc.com
Manufactures porcelain, stone, and metal tile.

Dex Studios
404-753-0600
www.dexstudios.com
Creates custom concrete sinks, tubs, and countertops.

Formica Corp.
513-786-3525
www.formica.com
Manufactures plastic laminate and solid-surfacing material.

Glidden
800-454-3336
www.glidden.com
Manufactures paint and related materials.

Island Stone North America
800-371-0001
www.islandstonena.com
Manufactures natural stone and glass tiles.

Jasba Tile
www.jasba.de/en
Manufactures tile.

Kohler
800-456-4537
www.kohler.com
Manufactures plumbing products.

Kraftmaid Cabinetry
440-632-5333
www.kraftmaid.com
Manufactures cabinetry.

Mannington, Inc.
856-935-3000
www.mannington.com
Manufactures resilient, engineered hardwood, porcelain, and plastic-laminate flooring.

Merillat
www.merillat.com
Manufactures cabinets.

Moen
800-289-6636
www.moen.com
Manufactures plumbing products.

Price Pfister, Inc.
800-732-8238
www.pricepfister.com
Manufactures faucets.

Remcraft Lighting Products
www.remcraft.com
Manufactures lighting fixtures.

Schonbek Worldwide Lighting Inc.
800-836-1892
www.schonbek.com
Manufactures crystal lighting fixtures.

Seagull Lighting Products, Inc.
856-764-0500
www.seagulllighting.com
Manufactures lighting fixtures.

Sensa by Cosentino
866-736-7270
www.sensagranite.com
Manufactures natural stone products.

Sherwin-Williams
www.sherwinwilliams.com
Manufactures paint.

Soft as Stone
218-834-7800
www.softasstone.com
Manufactures concrete products.

Stone Forest
888-682-2987
www.stoneforest.com
Manufactures stone products for kitchen and bath.

Stone Tile Depot
800-622-8708
www.stonetiledepot.com
Manufactures stone and tile.

Sub-Zero Freezer Co.
800-222-7820
www.subzero.com
Manufactures professional-style refrigeration
appliances.

Toto USA
770-282-8686
www.totousa.com
Manufactures toilets, sinks, and bathtubs.

Viking Range Corp.
www.vikingrange.com
Manufactures professional-style kitchen
appliances.

Wilsonart International
800-433-3222
www.wilsonart.com
Manufactures plastic-laminate countertops.

**Wolf Appliance Company,
a div. of Sub-Zero Freezer Co.**
www.wolfappliance.com
Manufactures professional-style cooking
appliances.

York Wallcoverings
717-846-4456
www.yorkwall.com
Manufactures borders and wallcoverings.

Your Color Source Studios
973-509-2304
http://yourcolorsource.info
A color consulting company for your home,
office, or business.

Zodiaq, a div. of DuPont
www.zodiaq.com
800-426-7426
Manufactures quartz composite material.

glossary

primary colors are equidistant, with secondary and tertiary colors between them.

Complementary colors Colors located opposite one another on the color wheel.

Contrast The art of assembling colors with different values and intensities to create visual harmony in a color scheme.

Cool colors The greens, blues, and violets.

Double-split complementaries Colors on either side of two complementary colors on the color wheel.

Earth tones The natural colors of earth; browns and beiges.

Eggshell A thin, brittle semimatte paint finish.

Glaze A paint or colorant mixed with a transparent medium and diluted with a thinner compatible with the medium.

Gloss A shiny finish that reflects the maximum amount of light.

Hue Synonym for color. Used to describe the color family to which a color belongs.

Intensity The brightness or dullness of a color. Also referred to as a color's purity or saturation.

Intermediate colors Colors made by mixing equal amounts of one primary and one secondary color, such as red-orange and blue-green.

Latex paints Paints that contain acrylic or vinyl resins or a combination of the two.

Advancing colors The warm colors. As with dark colors, they seem to advance toward you.

Alkyd paints Paints with artificial resins (alkyds) forming their binder; often imprecisely called "oil-based" paints. Alkyds have replaced the linseed oil formerly used as a binder in oil-based paint.

Analogous colors Any three colors located next to one another on the color wheel.

Chroma See *Intensity*.

Color scheme A group of colors used together to create visual harmony.

Color wheel A pie-shaped diagram showing the range and relationships of pigment. The three

Nap A soft or fuzzy surface on fabric (such as a paint-roller cover).

Pastel A color to which a lot of white has been added to make it very light in value.

Pigment The substances that give paint color. Pigments are derived from natural or synthetic materials that have been ground into fine powders.

Primary colors Red, yellow, and blue; the three colors in the visible spectrum that cannot be broken down into other colors. In various combinations and proportions, they make all other colors.

Quaternary colors Colors made by mixing two tertiary colors.

Receding colors The cool colors. They make surfaces seem farther from the eye.

Secondary colors Orange, green, and violet; the colors made by mixing equal amounts of two primary colors.

Semigloss A slightly lustrous finish that is light reflective and has an appearance somewhere between gloss and eggshell.

Shade A color to which black has been added to make it darker.

Sheen The quality of paint that reflects light.

Split complementary A color paired with the colors on either side of its complementary color on the color wheel.

Tertiary colors Colors made by combining equal amounts of two secondary colors.

Tint A color to which white has been added to make it lighter in value.

Tone A color to which gray has been added to change its value.

Triad Any three colors located equidistant from one another on the color wheel.

Value The lightness (tint or pastel) and darkness (shade) of a color.

Value scale A graphic tool used to show the range of values between pure white and true black.

Visible spectrum The bands of hues created when sunlight passes through a prism.

Warm colors Generally, the reds, oranges, and yellows; often including the browns.

index

photo credits

All stone/tile swatches courtesy of Stone Tile Depot, unless otherwise noted. All wood swatches courtesy of Merillat.

page 1: Mark Lohman, deisgn: Debbie Jones **page 3:** courtesy of Sherwin–Williams **page 4:** Tony Giammarino/Giammarino & Dworkin **page 6:** Beth Singer, design: Robin Wilson Architects, architect: CBI Architects **page 7:** Mark Lohman **page 8:** *top* Mark Samu, design: Sherill Canet *bottom* melabee m miller, design: Elizabeth Gillin **page 9:** Mark Samu, courtesy of Heart Magazines **page 10:** daviddduncanlivingston.com **pages 12–13:** Mark Samu **pages 14–15:** Tria Giovan **pages 16–19:** Mark Samu **page 20:** *top left* and *center* courtesy of Sherwin–Williams *top right* Mark Samu, builder: Dean Durst Construction *middle left* courtesy of Kohler *middle center* courtesy of Merillat *middle right* courtesy of Merillat *bottom left* courtesy of Kohler *bottom center* courtesy of Merillat *bottom right* Minh+Wass **page 24:** EVERETT & SOULE, design: Joan DesCombes, CKD, Architectural Artworks Incorporated **page 26:** Cameron Carothers Photography, design: Mark Cutler, Mark Cutler Design, Inc. **page 27:** Anne Gummerson, design: Gina Fitzsimmons, Fitzsimmons Design Associates **page 28:** courtesy of Merillat **page 29:** Dan Epstein, color consultant: Amy Wax/Your Color Source Studios, Inc. **page 30:** daviddduncanlivingston.com **page 31:** *left* courtesy of Seagull Lighting *center* Mark Samu *right* courtesy of Remcraft **page 32:** Mark Samu **page 33:** Mark Lohman **pages 34–35:** courtesy of Merillat **page 36:** Bob Greenspan, stylist: Susan Andrews **page 37:** courtesy of Mannington **pages 38–39:** Anne Gummerson, design: Gina Fitzsimmons, Fitzsimmons Design **page 40:** daviddduncanlivingston.com **page 41:** Jessie Walker, design: Jim & Jean Wagner, Woodfellows **page 42:** design: John A. Buscarello ASID **page 43:** EVERETT & SOULE, design: Joan DesCombes, CKD, Architectural Artworks Incorporated **page 44:** Mark Samu, design: Jean Stoffer **page 45:** EVERETT & SOULE, design: Joan DesCombes, CKD, Architectural Artworks Incorporated **page 46:** courtesy of Sensa by Cosentino **page 47:** Mark Samu, design: Lucianna Samu **page 48:** Sergio Fama, courtesy of Art & Maison Inc. **page 49:** courtesy of Zodiaq **page 50:** courtesy of Formica **page 51:** courtesy of Dupont **page 52:** courtesy of Corian **page 53:** courtesy of Formica **page 54:** courtesy of Wilsonart **page 55:** courtesy of Wilsonart **page 56:** daviddduncanlivingston.com **page 57:** Mark Samu, design: Bruce Nagle, A.I.A **page 58:** Mark Lohman **page 59:** www.carolynbates.com **page 60:** Anne Gummerson, architect: Brennan + Company Architects **page 61:** Mark Samu, design: Ken Kelly **page 62:** *top* Mark Samu *bottom* courtesy of Kohler **page 63:** Bob Greenspan, stylist: Susan Andrews **page 64:** courtesy of Stone Forest **page 65:** Mark Samu **page 66:** Mark Samu, design: Habitech **page 67:** courtesy of Price Pfister **page 68:** *top* Todd Caverly *bottom* courtesy of Moen **page 69:** courtesy of Viking **page 70:** courtesy of Exotic Metals **page 73:** *top left* Robert Kent Photography Canada *top right* Mark Lohman *bottom left* courtesy of Wilsonart *bottom right* Tria Giovan **page 74:** courtesy of Kohler **page 75:** Robert

Kent Photography Canada **page 76:** EVERETT & SOULE, design: Joan DesCombes, CKD, Architectural Artworks incorporated **page 77:** Mark Lohman **page 78:** Tria Giovan **page 79:** Mark Samu, courtesy of Hearst Magazines **page 80:** courtesy of Wilsonart **page 81:** Tony Giammarino/Giammarino & Dworkin, design: K. Kowach **page 82:** Mark Lohman, architect: Burdge & Associates **page 83:** Mark Lohman **page 84:** Mark Samu, courtesy of Hearst Magazines **page 85:** George Ross/CH **page 87:** *top left* courtesy of Kohler *top right* Mark Lohman, design: Susan Cohen Design *bottom left* design: Janice Stone Thomas, ASID, CKD *bottom right* Mark Lohman, design: Barclay Butera **page 88:** courtesy of Kohler **page 89:** Robert Perron **page 90:** courtesy of Kohler **page 91:** courtesy of Armstrong **page 92:** daviddduncanlivingston.com **page 93:** Mark Samu, design: Sam Scofield **page 94:** Mark Lohman, design: Susan Cohen Design **page 95:** Tria Giovan **page 96–97:** Mark Lohman, design: Barclay Butera **page 98:** daviddduncanlivingston.com **page 99:** design: Janice Stone Thomas, ASID, CKD **page 101:** *top left* Eric Roth, design: Benjamin Nutter *top right* courtesy of Sherwin–Williams *bottom left* daviddduncanlivingston.com *bottom right* courtesy of Armstrong **page 102:** courtesy of Seagull Lighting **page 103:** courtesy of Armstrong **page 104:** Dan Epstein **page 105:** Eric Roth, design: Benjamin Nutter **page 106:** courtesy of Armstrong **page 107:** courtesy of Sherwin–Williams **pages 108–109:** daviddduncanlivingston.com **page 110:** courtesy of Toto **page 111:** Phillip H. Ennis Photography **pages 112–113:** courtesy of Sherwin–Williams **pages 114–115:** courtesy of Sherwin– Williams **page 117:** *top left* Mark Samu, design: Ken Kelly **page** *top right* courtesy of KraftMaid *bottom left* courtesy of Merillat *bottom right* courtesy of Merillat **pages 118–119:** Mark Samu, design: Jean Stoffer **page 120–121:** Mark Samu, design: Ken Kelly **pages 122–123:** Mark Samu, design: Jean Stoffer **page 124:** courtesy of Island Stone **page 125:** courtesy of Merillat **page 126–127:** Mark Samu, design: The Tile Studio **page 128:** courtesy of Merillat; *top swatch* Home & Garden Editorial Services **page 129:** courtesy of Merillat **page 130:** courtesy of Merillat **page 131:** courtesy of Merillat **page 132:** *top* courtesy of KraftMaid; *top swatch* courtesy of Armstrong **page 133:** *top* courtesy of KraftMaid; top swatch Home & Garden Editorial Services **page 134:** Mark Samu, courtesy of Hearst Magazines **page 135:** Beth Singer, architect: Neumann & Smith Associates, design: Andrea Sachse **page 136:** *top* courtesy of Kohler; *bottom swatch* daviddduncanlivingston.com **page 137:** Glenn Moody, courtesy of Schonbek Worldwide Lighting, Inc. **page 139:** *top left* design: Brukoff Design Associates *top right* Mark Samu design: Bruce Nagel, A.I.A. *bottom left* Mark Samu, design: Lee Najman *bottom right* Peter Tata **page 140:** daviddduncanlivingston.com **page 141:** design: Michael Merrill Design Studio **page 142:** Mark Samu, design: Bruce Nagel, A.I.A. **page 143:** Anne Gummerson **page 144:** courtesy of Stone Age Designs, design: Scagliola Stone Collection by Thierry Francois **page 145:** EVERETT & SOULE, design: Joan DesCombes, CKD, Architectural Artworks,

Inc. **page 146:** *top* Mark Samu, design: Lucianna Samu; *bottom swatch* courtesy of Quickstep **page 147:** *top* Mark Samu, design: Lee Najman; *bottom swatch* Home & Garden Editorial Services **pages 148–149:** Peter Tata **pages 150–151:** *top both* design: Brukoff Design Associates; *center swatch* courtesy of Armstrong **page 152:** davidduncanlivingston.com **page 153:** *top* courtesy of Merillat; *bottom swatch* Home & Garden Editorial Services **page 155:** *top left* courtesy of Merillat *top right* courtesy of York Wallcoverings *both bottom* Eric Roth **pages 156–157:** courtesy of Toto **pages 158–159:** *top both* Eric Roth; *bottom right swatch* Home & Garden Editorial Services **page 160:** *top* Jessie Walker, architect: Lenore Bagelman, Full Circle Architects; *center swatch* Home & Garden Editorial Services **page 161:** Jessie Walker, design: Barbara Metzler **page 162:** Mark Samu, courtesy of Hearst Magazines **page 163:** Anne Gummerson **page 164:** Mark Lohman, design: Cheryl Hamilton–Gray **page 165:** *top* Jean Alsopp for American Clay; *bottom swatch* courtesy of Soft As Stone **page 166:** courtesy of Merillat **page 167:** courtesy of Merillat **page 168:** Elizabeth Whiting Associates **page 169:** courtesy of York Wallcoverings **page 171:** *top left* davidduncanlivingston.com *top right* davidduncanlivingston.com *bottom left* courtesy of Sherwin–Williams *bottom right* Beth Singer **page 172:** courtesy of DEX Studios **page 173:** courtesy of Sherwin–Williams **page 174:** davidduncanlivingston.com **page 175:** Mark Samu, design: Lucianna Samu **page 176:** Bob Greenspan, stylist: Susan Andrews **page 177:** courtesy of Exotic Metal Interiors **page 178:** Tria Giovan **page 179:** courtesy of Kohler **pages 180–181:** Beth Singer, cabinets & appliances: Trevarrow Inc., design/retail: DeGiulio Kitchen and Bath **page 182:** Beth Singer, cabinets & appliances: Trevarrow Inc., design: Pam Bytner Design **page 183:** Tony Giammarino/Giammarino & Dworkin, design: Kelly Stalls **page 184:** courtesy of Exotic Metal Interiors **page 185:** davidduncanlivingston.com **page 186:** davidduncanlivingston.com **page 187:** courtesy of Sherwin–Williams **pages 188–189:** Beth Singer **page 191:** *top left* Beth Singer, design: Kevin McManamon, architect: DesRosiers Architects *top right* courtesy of Crossville *bottom left* Beth Singer, design: Ausberg Interiors, architect: Young & Young Architects, builder: John Richards Homes *bottom right* Anne Gummerson **page 192:** Roy Inman, stylist: Susan Andrews **page 193:** davidduncanlivingston.com **page 194:** Mark Lohman **page 195:** courtesy of Crossville **page 196:** Beth Singer, design: Ausberg Interiors, architect: Young & Young Architects, builder: John Richards Homes **page 197:** Beth Singer, design: Kevin McManamon, architect: DesRosiers Architects **page 198–199:** *top both* Mark Samu, design: Ken Kelly; *bottom swatch* Home & Garden Editorial Services **pages 200–201:** courtesy of Kohler **page 202:** *top* Glenn Moody, courtesy of Schonbek Lighting, Inc.; *bottom swatch* davidduncanlivingston.com **page 203:** Anne Gummerson **page 205:** *top left* courtesy of Kohler *top right* Tria Giovan *bottom left* davidduncanlivingston.com *bottom right* courtesy of Merillat **page 206:** davidduncanlivingston.com **page 207:** Jessie Walker, design: Paulette O'Reilly Akins & Assoc. **page 208:** courtesy of Kohler

page 209: Tria Giovan **page 210:** courtesy of Merillat **page 211:** courtesy of Armstrong **pages 212–213:** davidduncanlivingston.com **page 214:** Mark Samu, design: The Tile Studio **page 215:** Mark Samu, design: Witt Construction **page 216:** design: Emily Castle, ASID, Castle Design **page 217:** Beth Singer **page 219:** *top left* Mark Samu, design: Deidre Gatta *top right* Amy Wax *bottom left* courtesy of Benjamin Moore *bottom right* Mark Samu **pages 220–224:** Mark Samu **page 225:** Mark Samu, design: Lee Najman **page 226:** Dan Epstein **page 227:** davidduncanlivingston.com **pages 228–229:** Amy Wax **pages 230–231:** Amy Wax **pages 232–233:** courtesy of Benjamin Moore **page 235:** *top left* Eric Roth *top right* courtesy of Merillat *bottom left* design: Lou Ann Bauer, ASID, Bauer Design *bottom right* davidduncanlivingston.com **page 236:** *top* design: Lou Ann Bauer, ASID, Bauer Design; *bottom swatch* courtesy of Expanko **page 237:** design: Cheng Design **page 238:** Jessie Walker **page 239:** Anne Gummerson, design: Cristine Wasiak **page 240:** Jessie Walker **page 241:** Mark Lohman, design: Debbie Jones **pages 242–243:** davidduncanlivingston.com **pages 244–245:** courtesy of Merillat **pages 246–247:** courtesy of Merillat **pages 248–249:** Mark Samu, design: Ken Kelly **pages 250–251:** Eric Roth **page 252:** courtesy of Glidden **page 253:** davidduncanlivingston.com **page 254:** Eric Roth **page 255:** Mark Samu, builder: Dean Durst Construction **page 256:** courtesy of Armstrong **page 257:** courtesy of Merillat **page 259:** *top left* courtesy of Jasba Tile *top right* courtesy of Kohler *bottom left* courtesy of Merillat *bottom right* design: Benning Design Assoc. **pages 260–261:** davidduncanlivingston.com **page 262:** *top* courtesy of Kohler; *top swatch* davidduncanlivingston.com **page 263:** courtesy of Merillat **page 264:** Thomas McConnell **page 265:** Sergio Fama, courtesy of Art & Maison, Inc. **pages 266–267:** courtesy of Merillat **pages 268–269:** EVERETT & SOULE, design: Joan DesCombes, CKD, Architectural Artworks Incorporated **page 270:** courtesy of Jasba Tile **page 271:** courtesy of Kohler **page 272:** Gabrielle Kessler, courtesy of Quintessentials, design: Elsa Kessler, cabinets: Brookhaven "Vista" **page 273:** Bob Greenspan, stylist: Susan Andrews **page 274:** Mark Lohman, architect: Abramson Tieger **page 275:** design: Benning Design Assoc. **page 277:** *top left* Beth Singer *top right* Mark Samu, design: Chester Winthrop *bottom left* Mark Samu, design: Kitchen Dimensions *bottom right* Jessie Walker, design: Gail Drury, Drury Design **page 278:** Nancy Elizabeth Hill **page 279:** davidduncanlivingston.com **page 280:** davidduncanlivingston.com **page 281:** courtesy of Armstrong **page 282–283:** Jessie Walker **page 284:** Mark Samu, design: Kitchen Dimensions **page 285:** Mark Samu, design: Jean Stoffer **page 286:** Mark Samu, design: Patrick Falco **page 287:** Jessie Walker, architect: Tom Greene Architect/Greene and Proppe Design Inc. **page 288:** Jessie Walker, design: Gail Drury, Drury Design **page 289:** courtesy of Wolf **page 290:** Beth Singer **page 291:** Mark Samu, design: Chester Winthrop **page 292:** Mark Samu, design: Ken Kelly **page 293:** Brian Vanden Brink, builder: Axel Berg **pages 296–297:** Amy Wax

Have a home improvement, decorating, or gardening project?

Look for these and other fine

Creative Homeowner books

wherever books are sold.

500 color photos. 224 pp.; 8½" x 10⅞"
$ 19.95 (US) $ 24.95 (CAN)
BOOK #: 279415

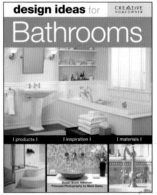

500 color photos. 224 pp.; 8½" x 10⅞"
$ 19.95 (US) $ 24.95 (CAN)
BOOK #: 279268

400 color photos. 304 pp.; 9¼" x 10⅞"
$ 24.95 (US) $ 29.95 (CAN)
BOOK #: 279679

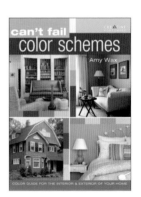

300 color photos. 304 pp.; 7" x 9¼"
$ 19.95 (US) $ 21.95 (CAN)
BOOK #: 279659

For more information and to order directly, go to
www.creativehomeowner.com